A HISTORY

OF

WONDERFUL INVENTIONS.

GUTTENBERG, SCHOEFFER, AND FUST, THE INVENTORS OF PRINTING.

A History

OF

WONDERFUL

INVENTIONS.

ILLUSTRATED WITH NUMEROUS ENGRAVINGS ON WOOD.

LONDON:

CHAPMAN AND HALL, 186 STRAND.

MDCCCXLIX.

CONTENTS.

PREFACE.

HE empire which man's "invention" has gained for him over nature is, already, great; but what it may be none can tell. The triumphs of science at present realized, may seem but trifles in the future. The human mind enlarges with its conquests, and each new step gives us encouragement to proceed with another, and we see not where a limit can be placed to the grand dominion man may in the end obtain. A period may arrive when even the Steam-engine may be derided as an imperfect piece of mechanism, and some discovery made that will enable man to wield equal force without the employment of its cumbrous bulk and expensive fabrication. Gas-light, the Printing Press and Printing Machine may, even, pass away into disuse by the institution of superior discoveries; and it may not

v

be affirmed that any one of the great instruments of present civilization, superb as they are accounted, are unlikely to disappear and give way to other creations of human invention. Electricity, especially, holds such a universe of mysterious power in itself, that we know not to what astonishing purposes it may be applied, even before the lapse of the present century. Printing can already be accomplished by it, and letters written and read in a few moments by those who are hundreds of miles from each other.

The glory of the future is only to be realized by maturing the grandeur of the present. It is by going on from the point already attained that a more splendid and perfect future is to be reached. Whoever, then, in his youth vows a life-long service to knowledge, or "girds up his loins" with a resolve to become her devoted and untiring disciple, and thus enters into the ranks of science to learn what is now known, increases the probability of science being perfected, inasmuch as new thought and new ardour leads to new invention. " Men's minds are as various as their faces," is an old adage ; and every new mind brought within the focal light of science is likely to be enkindled with some new thought by its intellectual beam. Students are what science now requires—young, ardent, never-wearying students, to urge on the glowing process of discovery. Every one who devotes himself to knowledge may become a benefactor of mankind ; for whoever increases its empire enlarges human happiness, and helps to quell the reign of evil and suffering.

Let the young reader, then, strengthen his determination to enlist under the peaceful but ennobling banner of science, by the remembrance that all its great names are held to be more honourable than the military conqueror, because the triumphs of knowledge and invention are gained without bloodshed, and it is their inevitable tendency to bring war to an end. The communication of mutual advantage by the diffusion of commerce; the perception of such advantage by the exchange of thought, of manufacture, of the comforts and refinements of existence, and by the cultivation of fraternal good-will, are certain results of the increase of science. Who, then, would be slack to enrol himself her disciple while life is young, and there is a prospect of blessing mankind by entering her service? Who would yield to sloth, or dissipate his powers in empty folly, when greater fame may be won, for aught he knows to the contrary, even by his devoted thought, for universal humanity, than has been awarded to Guttemberg or Caxton, Galileo or Copernicus, or even to a Newton, Herschel, Davy, or Watt?

Young reader, the glorious path is open: none can prevent your entering it; there needs but patience and resolution.

WONDERFUL INVENTIONS.

THE MARINER'S COMPASS.

It is nearly two thousand years since Julius Cæsar first landed from his Roman galley on the English coast. It was on a fine morning in August—just about the time that the ancient Britons were gathering in their corn-harvest—when the Roman legions first saw the British war-chariots, with the sharp scythes projecting from their wheels, as they went thundering along the sandy beach below the cliffs of Dover; and great must have been their astonishment, as they gazed from the decks of their high galleys, on the half naked, long-

1

haired Britons, some of whom were paddling their coracles, or boats, which were made of osiers, covered with the hides of oxen, and in which they seldom ventured far from the shore.

Although it was not until centuries after this period that the compass was known in Britain, the Greeks and Romans were aware, long before the time of Cæsar, that an island celebrated for its tin lay somewhere on the north or north-west of Europe. The Greeks made many attempts to discover the Cassiterides, or islands of tin, as they called them. It appears, however, that they kept along the coast of Normandy and France, and were afraid to venture across our stormy channel, for they had no magnet to steer by. The Phœnicians, who were the earliest traders that visited England, baffled all inquiries that the Greeks made as to the situation of these celebrated islands, and had for centuries all the traffic in tin to themselves. It was in vain that the Greeks sent out ships to discover where these early Phœnician voyagers landed ; the latter ran their vessels ashore on the coast of France, and would not steer across the English Channel until the Greeks had departed ; nor does the secret of the Phœnicians appear to have been discovered until Julius Cæsar invaded Britain.

It will be readily perceived, by referring to a map of Europe, that the magnet was not necessary as a guide from the coast of France to England, as, on a clear day, our white island-cliffs may be seen from the opposite shore, and a few hours would be sufficient to cross the narrow sea which divides the two countries. Until the galleys ventured over, they would there-fore keep in sight of the shore, and glide safely from headland to headland as they crept along the opposite coast.

In those early times chance or accident, no doubt, led to the discovery of more distant countries. A vessel might be borne along by a heavy wind, and in dark, cloudy, or tempestuous weather, when the sun did not appear, these early mariners would neither be able to distinguish the east from the west, nor

2

the north from the south; thus they would be compelled to sail along for days, ignorant of what latitude they were in, until they at last reached land; nor would they then be able to tell in what quarter lay the country they had left behind. Hundreds, no doubt, were lost, who were thus driven out into these unknown and perilous seas without either map or chart, or any guide by which to steer to the right or left. Backwards and forwards would they be carried by the winds and currents, and when the sun shone not, and no star appeared upon the blue front of Heaven, they might as well have been launched upon the immensity of space where profound silence ever reigns, for it would have been a hopeless task for them ·to find their way back again over those unknown and mastless seas.

The magnet, or loadstone—that invisible bridge which spans from continent to continent, and makes the path over the ocean plain as a broad highway—is a dark greyish looking mineral, that possesses the property of attracting towards itself anything that has either iron or steel in its composition, and is likewise capable of communicating the same power of attraction to either of these metals. These qualities of the magnet were well-known to the ancient Greeks, who, Pliny tells us, gave the name "Magnet" to the rock near Magnesia, a city of Lydia, in Asia Minor; and the ancient poet Hesiod also makes use of the term "magnet stone."

At what period that more important property of the magnet, "polarity," or its disposition to turn to the north and south poles of the earth, was first discovered, is not known. The Greeks and Romans were, alike, ignorant of it; and thus, the more distant portions of the globe remained unknown to these enterprizing nations. Among the Chinese, however — that strange people who, like the monuments in eastern climes, seem to remain for ages unchanged either in aspect or character — the magnet appears to have been well understood from a very remote date; and to have been used for the purposes of direction, in most of the leading countries of Asia, including Japan, as well as China, India, and even Arabia. And it is not very unlikely that the leading knowledge of it in Europe, like the art of medicine, was first derived from the Moors; for we find a vague and uncertain acquaintance with it about two centuries after their attacks upon the Goths in Spain.

The earliest notice of the magnet, in the Chinese records, relates to a period of 2,634 years before the birth of our Saviour. This is a questionable date; yet, though we cannot fix the circumstance alluded to with any certainty, there can be no doubt but that the native accounts refer to very ancient times. The Jesuit missionaries, who went to China in the seventeenth century, were rigorous investigators of its claims to such high antiquity; and the celebrated German scholar, Klaproth, as well as Mr. Davis, have both given translations of the passage in which the first application of the magnet is mentioned.

No further notice of the compass is found in the books of China, so far as they have come to the knowledge of Europeans, until about the close of the third century of the Christian era, where, in the dictionary of Poi-wen-yeu-fou, it is stated, "that ships were then directed to the south by the needle."

Many circumstances contribute to the impression that the mariner's compass was first made known in Europe through the communication of the Moorish invaders of Spain, although the knowledge of it has been brought direct from China; first through Marco Polo himself, the celebrated traveller in Cathay, and afterwards by Dr. Gilbert, the physician to Queen Elizabeth. In 1718 a book was published in Paris by Eusebius Renandof, which gives an account of the journey of two Mahommedan travellers in Syria in the ninth century. This book is translated from an Arabic manuscript, which is said to bear all the marks of authenticity: in this it is stated, that at that time the Chinese traded in ships to the Persian Gulf and the Red Sea;

4

and it is hardly possible that they could have constantly performed such long voyages without the aid of a compass. Among the Arabs, it was chiefly used by the explorers of new countries in tracking their way across the sandy deserts, or over the unknown prairie; and we may readily picture to ourselves the turbaned merchant of the olden time, with stout heart and enterprising spirit, sallying forth from his city home, and finding, after a few day's journey, nothing but an apparently endless plain stretching far before him, across which, with the aid of his compass, he would boldly prepare to take his way with his attendants and his camels, in the sure hope of reaching the distant city to which he was journeying.

The following description, translated from the Arabic manuscript alluded to, gives a certain intimation of the knowledge of the properties of the magnet on the eastern seas long before it was generally used in Europe: —

"The captains who navigate the Syrian Sea, when the night is so dark as to conceal from view the stars which might direct their course, according to the position of the four cardinal points, take a basin full of water, which they shelter from the wind by placing it in the interior of the vessel. They then drive a needle into a wooden peg or corn stalk, so as to form the shape of a cross, and throw it into the basin of water prepared for the purpose, on the surface of which it floats. They afterwards take a loadstone about the size of the palm of the hand or even smaller, bring it to the surface of the water, give to their hands a rotatory motion towards the right, so that the needle turns round, and then suddenly and quickly withdraw their hands, when the two points of the needle face the north and the south."

An attempt has been made by Professor Hansteen to establish the knowledge of the polarity of the magnet, and its use, among the Norwegians, in the eleventh century; but the work which he quotes in support of his opinion, although unques-

5

tionably of ancient date, appears to have been tampered with, and the passage on which he relies is not to be found in three of the manuscript copies. There are, indeed, doubts whether the book itself is of older date than the fourteenth century. The compass is, however, minutely described in the satire entitled "La Bible," which was written by Guyot de Provins, and appeared about the year 1190; but it is evident, from the terms used by him, that it was an instrument but little known, and which had only lately been introduced into Europe. Cardinal Vitrey and Vincent de Beauvais, who were attached to the French army in the crusades, both speak of the compass as a great curiosity which they had seen in the East. De Provins was a minstrel; and as he wrote only some twenty or five-and-twenty years before the cardinal, there is great probability that he obtained his knowledge of the polarity of the magnet, and its application to the purposes of direction, from the same part of the world. It is indeed just such a discovery as was likely to emanate from Arabian genius; and as one reads the statements of these old chroniclers, they carry the mind back to the day of glaive and helm, and the imagination pictures the wild scenery of a Syrian landscape, where a party of bewildered travellers, composed of such as the three persons we have mentioned, are seated by the side of some out-pouring fount, which, as it wells through the green sward, reflects in its crystal surface the rich hues of an eastern clime. Around are scattered the towering and broken hills, clad with the scanty foliage of climbing shrubs, and, now and then, a dark luxuriant cedar of mighty growth. There, seated beneath a lofty rock, with its rude broken front stained by the hues of centuries, and here and there green with vegetation, are the three individuals who first gave authentic information to Europe of that invention which was destined to set at nought utterness of darkness, and fog, and wind, and rain, and unite as it were together the most distant families of the earth. There sits the

cardinal, half soldier, half priest, clad in his tonsure, and girt
with his two-handed sword; De Beauvais, with helm by
his side, guarded at all points by his supple chain-armour;
and De Provins, who has just
laid aside the lute with which
he had beguiled his hearers and
the time, listening to the strange
accounts of the dark-bearded
and turbaned traveller, who, with
the small compass in his hand,
is pointing to the direction they
must take to rejoin their friends.

Thus much appears to be established, that before the third
crusade the knowledge of the use of the compass for land purposes had been obtained from the East, and that by the year

1269 it was common in Europe. Its use for the purpose of navigation, in this part of the world, was first ascribed to Flavio Gioja, a Neapolitan, born at Amalfi, and its application was said to have been made about the beginning of the fourteenth century. But it is evident, from what has been already observed, that it was known, as a nautical instrument, long before his period; and there is evidence in the "Tresor" of Brunetto, the master of the great Italian poet Dante, that it was not a rarity in his time. How Gioja's name became associated so prominently with the history of the compass, does not appear; but it is probable that he either greatly improved it by the appendage of the card, or brought it into more general use.

We do not find the magnet mentioned earlier in our English records than the reign of Edward III.; it was then known by the name of the "sail-stone," or "adamant," and the compass was called the sailing-needles, or dial, though it is long after this period before we find the word compass. A ship called the Plenty sailed from Hull in 1338, and we find that she was steered by the sailing-stone. In 1345, that is, five hundred years ago, another entry occurs, which states that one of the King's ships, called the George, brought over sixteen horologies from Sluys in Normandy, and that money had been paid at the same place for twelve stones, called adamants or sail-stones, and for "*repairing divers instruments pertaining to a ship.*"

The construction of the mariner's compass is as follows:— A magnetized needle is balanced on a pivot raised from a circular card, on which the points of the compass are described; the chief of them, or the cardinal points, as they are termed— from the word *carda*, a hinge or pivot—showing those which are intermediate between the east, west, north, and south. This card is also connected sideways by similar pivots to a frame formed of what are called *concentric* circles. These are represented by two hoops, placed so as to cross each other, and the card is suspended just in the centre of the two, so that which-

8

ever way the vessel may lurch, the card is always in an horizontal position, and certain to point the true direction of the head of the ship. The concentric circles, or hoops, are termed *gimbals* or *gymbals*, and they are generally allowed to have been the invention of an Englishman, though there appears to be no evidence of the fact.

By whom the marking of the points was introduced is not known. The French have laid claim to the invention, and some of their authors have asserted that the marking of the four cardinal points was merely a modification of their *fleur-de-lis;* but a contrary question has been raised on the other hand, and a supposition has been started that the fleur-de-lis itself is only a modification of the *mouasala*, or dart, which the Arabs used to denote the direction of the needle, and which is employed to point out the north on our maps at the present time. Chaucer, who died in 1400, mentions the compass ; and states, that the sailors reckon thirty-two points of the horizon, which is the present division of the card.

The discovery of the "declination of the needle," or that deviation from the true north and south which its poles evince, has been ascribed to an Englishman. It is unlikely that it could remain unknown long after the compass had been used as a nautical instrument in high latitudes. That Columbus was acquainted with it is evident from a passage in his life written by his son; and, in all probability, it proved one of the greatest difficulties with which he had to contend, especially as it is now known to vary in the different parts of the world, and is of necessity influenced by "terrestial magnetism," or the magnetism of the earth.

The words "terrestial magnetism" lead us, at once, to the most absorbing scientific question of the present day; but we must use the utmost brevity in touching upon it. What was called the "igneous theory," or doctrine of a central fire within the earth, has now given way to the belief, among philosophers,

9

that changes in the temperature of the air, and various other natural phenomena, are attributable to the earth's magnetic power. Professor Faraday, among Englishmen, has substantiated the grand fact, that the earth is one vast magnet; and Gauss, of Gottingen, computes the magnetic power of each cubic yard of the earth to be equal to that of six steel magnets, each of one pound weight.

It is also ascertained that magnetic currents are continually passing from the south to the north pole, through and around the earth. All the phenomena attributed to fire may be produced by these magnetic currents, while it would be difficult to admit the existence of interior fires unsupplied with the oxygen of the atmosphere. Now, not only are the causes of earthquakes, and of the action of volcanoes, rendered explicable by these discoveries; but the establishment of the fact that the electric currents are perpetually passing from the south to the north pole, through and around the earth, strips the "dip," or "declination of the needle" of the mystery it has so long worn.

In consequence of these influences there is a natural depression at that end of a magnetic needle, when it is suspended on its pivot, towards which the current of magnetism, as it may be called, is driven. This has been termed the *dip;* and many elaborate and careful experiments have been tried to ascertain precisely the amount of this dip; and through the observations made during these experiments, it has been discovered that it varies, and that a magnetic needle oscillates, to a certain extent, every twenty-four hours. In order to avoid the mischief that might arise if this were not allowed for, the magnetic needle of the mariner's compass is always suspended out of the mechanical centre of gravity.

If a needle, or other magnetized substance, be fixed on the top of a piece of cork, which is then placed on the surface of water, and left to float unrestrained, it will be found that one end of the needle will turn till it points nearly towards the

10

north. This is the point at which the current enters the needle; the other end will of course point nearly towards the south; and if the cork be turned round, so as to direct the needle to the points opposite to those towards which it was naturally directed, it will, as soon as it is released from compulsion, again assume the position which it previously held. This at once explains the reason why the mariner can direct his ship across the waves, even in the darkest night and among the remotest regions, as by his compass he can always ascertain the course his vessel is taking, and by altering the bearing of the helm, and shifting his sails, he keeps his ship constantly under command, and guides her to her destined haven.

LIGHTHOUSES.

THERE is another facility given to the mariner, which, if
not so absolutely necessary to his progress as the compass,
tends to relieve him from much of that danger to which he is
continually exposed. This is the lighthouse erected along the
sea-coast, or on some rock far away from the shore, over which the
waves of the tempestuous ocean are unceasingly rolling, and
which is placed there to warn passing or approaching vessels of
shoals or other dangers that might cause their destruction. A few
centuries ago, in and around England the sea and the land were
alike dark. The bluff headlands of our coast looked over the
sunken rocks, and the dangerous shoals — the shifting sea-
sands had no friendly light to throw its golden streak upon the
boiling eddies, or warn the traveller where Death was ever

12

waiting for his prey. The billows broke, booming upon the beach, over the wrecked vessel; for then, instead of life-boats manned with brave men, who from childhood have been familiar with the dangers of the deep, there were cruel wreckers prowling upon the shore in the darkness, ready to slay and rob the half-drowned mariners rather than to rescue them.

One of the earliest lighthouses of which we have any account was built on a rock called Pharos, opposite the city of Alexandria, about the year 283 B.C., in the time of Ptolemy Philadelphus, king of Egypt. This island was something short of a mile from the city, to which it was joined by a causeway, and upon the rock, of which it chiefly consists, Sostratus, the son of Dexiphanes, built a tower of white marble, which was considered one of the seven wonders of the world. It had several stories one above another, adorned with columns and balustrades, and galleries, formed of the whitest marble, wrought into the most beautiful workmanship. On the top, fires were kept constantly burning to direct sailors how to gain the harbour of Alexandria, which was at that time exceedingly difficult of access. And such was the splendour of the light, that it is said to have been visible at the distance of nearly a hundred miles, a fact that appears to be incredible. No pains were spared to render this tower as substantial and beautiful as possible, and the erection is calculated to have cost as much as eight hundred talents, which, if they are to be considered as Attic talents, were equal to £165,000 of our money, or if they were Egyptian coins, would amount in value to more than £300,000 sterling. Its fame indeed became so general, that its name was adopted as a generic term, and every lighthouse was afterwards known, almost till our own day, by the appellation of *Pharos*.

As the arts improved, so did the construction of these edifices progress, until one of the greatest accomplishments of engineering skill, ever attempted upon such works, was exhibited

13

in the construction of the Eddystone Lighthouse, which is, indeed, much more entitled than the Pharos of Alexandria to be considered one of the wonders of the world. The rock on which this tower is built is placed about twelve miles southwest of Plymouth, and consists of a series of submarine cliffs, stretching from the west side (which is so precipitous that the largest ship can ride close beside them) in an easterly direction, for nearly half a mile. At the distance of about a quarter of a mile more is another rock, so that a more dangerous marine locality can hardly be imagined. Both these rocks had proved the cause of many fatal shipwrecks, and it was at last resolved to make an attempt to obviate the danger. In the year 1696, a gentleman of Essex, named Winstanley, who had a turn for architecture and mechanics, was engaged to erect a lighthouse upon the Eddystone rock, and in four years he completed it. It did not, however, stand long, for while some repairs were in progress under his direction in 1703, on the 26th November, a violent hurricane came on which blew the lighthouse down, and Mr. Winstanley and all his workmen perished—nothing remaining of the edifice but a few stones and a piece of iron chain.

In the spring of 1706 an Act of Parliament was obtained for rebuilding the lighthouse, and a gentleman named Rudyerd, a silk mercer, was the engineer engaged. He placed five courses of heavy stones upon the rock, and then erected a superstructure of wood. The lighthouse on the Bell Rock, off the coast of Fife, and the one placed at the entrance of the Mersey on the Black Rock, are similarly constructed, so that there seemed to be good reason for adopting the principle. Mr. Smeaton thought that the work was done in a masterly and effective manner ; but in 1755 the edifice was destroyed by fire, and he was next retained as the engineer for this important building.

The result of his labours has justly been considered worthy of the admiration of the world, for it is distinguished alike for

14

THE EDDYSTONE LIGHTHOUSE.

its strength, durability, and beauty of form. The base of the tower is about twenty-six feet nine inches in diameter, and the masonry is so formed as to be a part of the solid rock, to the height of thirteen feet above the surface, where the diameter is diminished to nineteen feet and a half. The tower then rises in a gradually diminishing curve to the height of eighty-five feet, including the lantern, which is twenty-four feet high. The upper extremity is finished by a cornice, a balustrade being placed around the base of the lantern for use as well as ornament.

The tower is furnished with a door and windows, and the whole edifice outside bears the graceful outline of the trunk of a mighty tree, combining lightness with elegance and strength.

15

Mr. Smeaton commenced his labours in 1756, and completed the building in four years. Before commencing operations he took accurate drawings of the exterior of the rock; and the stones, which were brought from the striking and romantic district of Dartmoor, were all formed to fit into its crevices, and so prepared as to be dovetailed together, and strung by oaken plugs. When put into their places, and then firmly cemented, the whole seemed to form, and does indeed constitute, a part of the solid rock.

The sand-bank off the coast of Ramsgate, known by the name of the Goodwin Sands, is a far more dangerous foe to the mariner than the Eddystone rocks ever were before any friendly lighthouse rose above the waters, and pointed out to approaching vessels the dangers by which they were beset. Situated as it is in the main track of that watery highway along which there ever moves to and fro the chief part of the commerce of the world — there, perhaps, more noble ships have foundered than on any other sand-bank in the ocean. At one moment a ship may be in ten fathoms soundings, and in the next strike upon this treacherous shoal, where her destruction is inevitable. To guard against this fearful danger, various efforts have been made to plant some beacon on these sands, which should warn the seaman of the perils which await him, but one after another, the waves have washed away the various structures which have been erected for this purpose. No solid foundation could be found—every attempt failed. So deep down under the floor of the ocean do the sands extend that no plummet could ever sound their depth. Dangerous as these sands are, which stretch over an extent of nearly ten miles, they still form a safe shield to the shore, by receiving the first burst of those mighty waves which are raised by the easterly winds. Thus they become a barrier against the billows that would otherwise be rolled upon the beach, and render the Downs a safe anchorage-ground, which, but for this,

16

would be as stormy and unsafe for a fleet to ride at anchor in as the most perilous part of the channel. A floating light has for some time been placed on the east side of the northern head of these dangerous sands, and has been instrumental in saving many a goodly vessel from foundering. There are signs along the coast which clearly point out traces of the ocean having flowed many yards higher than it does now, and at that remote period of time these ancient sands would be buried beneath the waves, instead of visible, as great portions of them are at low water, when you may venture upon them with safety; but when the tide and sea sets in they become soft, and woe to the adventurer that remains!—a grave, whose bottom has never yet been fathomed, would be his lot.

Of course the one grand object in the construction of a lighthouse is, that it shall be enabled to display as large and intense a light as possible. On the several coasts of the British islands the usual plan adopted is to place an argand burner in the focus of a parabolic reflector; that is, a reflector something in the shape of the round end of half an egg, which reflector is composed of highly-polished silver, coated and strengthened by copper.

On the French and Dutch coasts the reflector is generally made of glass, formed so as to have circle after circle outside of each other, and thus to obtain a condensing power. When the light is required to be cast far over the water, the English light, which is obtained by *reflection*, is considered the best, as it causes the rays to be more distributed. But there are difficulties connected with it; for as it is necessary, not only to render the several lights along the same coast different in appearance from each other, but also to accumulate the power of some, a number of reflectors is frequently used instead of one, and these require much cleaning when they are made of metal.

The intensity of the French lights is obtained by *refraction*, and thus the rays of light being interlaced, as it may be termed, with each other, their power is greater within a short distance; but their force cannot be thrown so far over the ocean as the rays from the English lights.

On the British coasts there are now, including floating lights, of which that placed at the Nore is an admirable example, nearly two hundred lighthouses. On the northern and western coasts of France there are eighty-nine lights; and the Dutch have twenty-six lights, altogether, on their sea-coast and on the shores of the Zuyder Zee.

These lights are maintained by a small charge levied on the tonnage of all vessels approaching or passing them, which varies from a farthing to twopence the ton. The total amount collected in this way, from British lighthouses, is about £250,000 a year, the cost of keeping them up being somewhere about a third of that amount, thus leaving a considerable sum for future improvements.

SECTIONAL VIEW OF EDDYSTONE LIGHTHOUSE.

GUNPOWDER AND GUN-COTTON.

BEFORE the invention of gunpowder, a battle-field presented a very different appearance to what it does now. There was then no heavy veil of smoke hanging over it and obscuring the banners on which the arms of the knights were emblazoned; the dancing plume, the glittering helmet, and the dazzling array of men in armour were on each side visible. Whether the warrior struck with his uplifted battle-axe, or made a plunge with his sharp-headed and long-shafted spear, or raising his gauntleted hand, thrust his long straight double-edged sword between the bars of his opponent's vizor, he saw the point at which he aimed, and stood face to face with the enemy to whom he was opposed. Each was alike prepared to attack or defend, and no random bullet came whizzing through the clouded canopy of smoke, levelling alike the strong and the weak, the brave and the base, and rendering neither determined courage nor skilful defence of any avail. The thundering cannon and the death-dealing bullet laid low the plumed and knightly head of chivalry; and the iron arm of a Cœur de Lion, that was ever foremost to hew its way into the enemy's ranks, with the ponderous battle-axe chained to its wrist, might have been shattered by the hand of the puniest peasant that trembled as it pulled the trigger, had the lion-hearted king lived when the bullet came, without a human hand to conduct it, from the muzzle of the firelock. · Those single combats, which our early bards loved to celebrate in their rude martial ballads, were then at an end; the standard could no longer be seen rocking and reeling above the heads of the combatants, and telling as it rose and fell the very spot where the heart of battle beat : for gunpowder came in and sent its blackening smoke over all this splendour, and under its clouded covering Death walked forth unperceived, levelling all alike, and making no distinction between cowardice and valour. War was at once shorn of all its false charms, and many there were who regretted the stern old days when men fought shield to shield and hand to hand, and who exclaimed with Shakspere,—

> " —— that it was great pity, so it was,
> That villanous saltpetre should be digged
> Out of the bowels of the harmless earth,
> Which many a good tall fellow had destroyed
> So cowardly."

The jousts and tournaments in which lances were shivered, and over which queens and titled ladies presided, were at an end. The fabled giants dwindled to dwarfs, for even fancy could not create a monster so tall that the bullet could not reach him. All these old fictions faded away when gunpowder was introduced.

A modern battle-field is the most terrible spectacle that can be contemplated. Tens and hundreds of thousands of men, intent on destruction, are pitted together, rank opposed to

20

rank, while horses and riders rush headlong upon each other, with glaring eyes and compressed lips. The air is filled with dark sulphureous smoke, through which the forked flames of the cannon are every moment flashing, as they send forth their dreadful messengers of death,—the rushing of mighty squadrons,—the loud clangour of arms, heard even amid the roar of the artillery, as at brief intervals its loud reports crash like some terrible thunder-clap,—the rapid volleys of the musketry filling up with their incessant rattle that discordant din which is only broken by the imprecations of enraged men, the screams of anguish, and the groans of the dying; these, with their fearful accessories, constitute a scene which is alike revolting to the principles of humanity, as it is opposed to the doctrines of our religion.

Yet, dreadful as is a scene like this, there is little doubt but that the principal agent through which it is enacted—gunpowder—has been instrumental in reducing the horrors of warfare, and saving human life: that there is less of that savage butchery and personal revenge which stained the battle-fields of ancient times. Allowing for the conflicting statements on both sides, it would seem that at the battle of Waterloo somewhere about two hundred thousand men were opposed to each other, and during a conflict of almost unexampled severity, which lasted from eleven o'clock in the morning till night had set in, the killed and wounded were estimated at twenty thousand; while in the battle fought by Henry V. with the French on the plains of Agincourt, the loss of life was proportionably much greater; and in the great battle fought at Lowton in Yorkshire, between the Yorkists and Lancasterians, which secured Edward IV. on the throne of England, upwards of forty thousand of the combatants perished, although the numbers of the contending armies did not exceed the strength of the French troops alone engaged at Waterloo.

Nor has the use of gunpowder been less instrumental in

abating the angry passions and the demoniacal hatred engendered in that most dreadful of all human scourges, war, than it has been useful in reducing the number of its victims. In the warfare of the ancients, and of those who lived in what are called the middle ages (with the exception of the archers, and they, in general, formed but a small portion of any army), the men opposed to each other, as we have already described, fought hand to hand. Thus, when any one received a wound, he most likely saw by whom it was inflicted, and viewing his opponent with an intense degree of malevolence, returned the injury, when in his power, with a proportionate ill-will. So would what we call our English spirit of "fair play" have a check in this feeling of personal revenge. But now the greater part of every battle is fought by men who have no opportunity of perceiving by whom they are wounded or hurt; and being thus less prompted by personal feeling, the termination of an engagement shows a far greater degree of humanity than was formerly known; and the instances are even numerous where those who but an hour or a few minutes before were at deadly strife, have evinced the noblest generosity in allaying the sufferings of each other.

Cruel as war is, it is surely better to end it quickly than to prolong it. To do in a few hours what might be continued for days, bad as it is, is to shorten human suffering; and we may hope at last that the more powerful the agent of destruction, the more effective it will be found for the shortening, and perhaps in time the prevention of war altogether.

An instance of this was given by the naval force under the command of Sir R. Stopford, who, in 1841, was sent to rescue Syria from the power of Mohammed Ali, the Pacha of Egypt. After taking the commercial town of Beyrout, this force sailed to bombard the town of St. Jean D'Acre, then considered one of the strongest fortresses in the world. It had been fortified with the utmost care, and was considered by those who defended

22

it as almost impregnable. But Sir Robert dispatched a few of his line-of-battle ships to silence the cannon on the walls, while, with the steam frigates under his command, he kept further from shore, and threw, from the mortars on board of his vessels, large shells into the place.

The fire was close and effective: and the guns of one of the seventy-fours were so placed, that the whole of her broadside was poured into one small space, described by an eye-witness as not more than ten feet square; and all the balls striking nearly at the same instant, the force of the blow was so irresistible that the solid masonry cracked, yielded, and with a thundering crash finally fell down into fragments, leaving a breach sufficiently wide enough for the assailants to enter the town.

In the meantime the admiral contrived to ply the defenders with volleys of shells from the steam frigates; and one of these breaking through the roof of an encased building, there burst. This chanced to be the magazine, where all the ammunition of the place was deposited. The contents immediately exploded; and one of the most sublime and awful sights that even the terrible machinery of war can produce was witnessed, as the vast mass of the building, with the bodies of seventeen hundred men, was driven, like the outpouring of a volcano, high and reddening into the air. The whole town was for a while enveloped in terrific darkness; and when the cause and the effect of the accident were perceived, it was considered useless to continue the contest: and thus, though at a great sacrifice, in three hours, was brought to a conclusion a war which might have continued for months or years, and which would have covered whole provinces and countries with desolation.

Cannons, or guns, as they are more commonly called, are distinguished by the weight of the ball which they are capable of discharging. Thus we have 68-pounders, 32-pounders, 24-pounders, 18-pounders, and the lighter field-

23

pieces, from 4 to 12-pounders. The quantity of powder used for the discharge of the several pieces in general warfare is— for common brass and iron guns, *one-third* the weight of powder to the ball, whatever the weight of the latter may be; for brass *howitzers*, which are the same in shape nearly as common cannon, being larger in the bore or inside and shorter in length, the quantity of powder used is *one-ninth* the weight of the ball; while in the firing of *carronades*, a still shorter and wider piece, the quantity of powder used is only *one-twelfth* the weight of the ball, being, as you will perceive, considerably less than what is used for common cannons.

By the use of something like this proportion, in several experiments which have been made, both at Woolwich and in France, where the several guns were directed *point blank*, that is, so as to fire the ball perfectly straight at the object aimed at, the largest class of cannon-balls was carried a range of 360 yards, and 18-pounders as far as 400 yards, from iron guns;—from brass guns, a 12-pound shot was sent 330 yards, and a 3-pound shot 350 yards; while from carronades, the range of shot was, of 68-pounders 300 yards, of a 42-pound shot 270 yards, a 24-pound 250 yards, and of a 12-pound shot 230 yards. In general warfare, when what is called *ricochet* practice is often used, the most effective distances at which cannon can be used, is from 500 to 600 yards, or from a quarter to half a mile. At the battle of Waterloo, the brigades of artillery were stationed about half a mile from each other. Cannon and shells, however, can be thrown with effect to the distance of a mile and a half to two miles. From its destructive power it will naturally be supposed that some efforts have been made to ascertain what the force of gunpowder is when it causes a ball to strike any object.

The experiments have been numerous, and in Sir Howard Douglas's "Treatise on Naval Gunnery," it is recorded that several trials were made; in one instance, by firing an 18-pounder

24

shot into a butt made of beams of oak, when the charges were 6 lbs. of powder, 3 lbs., 2¼ lbs., and 1 lb., the respective depths of the penetration were 42 inches, 30 inches, 28 inches, and 15 inches, and the velocities at which the balls flew were 1600 feet in a second, 1140 feet, 1024 feet, and 656 feet. In 1835, in some experiments made at Woolwich, where balls were fired at a wall of concrete, that is, a composition of stone, made into a kind of cement, which hardens as it sets till it is harder than stone itself, two 24 lb. shot fired at a velocity of 1390 feet in a second, penetrated the wall to the depth of 3 feet 10 inches. When fired into wood, on account of the resistance of the fibres, which are driven forward by the ball, the depth reached by a large quantity of powder, exhibits less than the usual force. The knowledge of these facts is of great importance, as it enables engineers to judge of the strength of the erections constructed to resist the power of cannon, and thus preserve the lives and property of persons in besieged places. It should be further observed that in attacking fortifications, it is always necessary to elevate the mouths of the pieces, which fire the shot and shells, to the extent of from six to nine degrees of the arch of the horizon, the reason of which shall be explained hereafter.

Not only, however, is gunpowder employed in the discharge of deadly missiles above ground, but it is used to undermine the works of towns, and thus level their defences to allow the besiegers to enter. These mines which are formed for the defence of towns, are called *defensive* mines, and those formed by their opponents *offensive* mines.

There were formerly two kinds of mines used in the attack of a fortress. One was a subterranean passage, run under the walls, and charged with gunpowder, which being exploded, enabled the besiegers to enter, and thus attack the defenders in the very heart of their stronghold. The other was employed to demolish the walls themselves, and thus enable the attacking force to bring all their power within the town, through the breach they had succeeded in making.

In the former case the business was to drive an underground way, or gallery as it was called, and at the end to deposit a quantity of combustible matter, which, being exploded at a certain time, opened the way for those attacking to enter the fortress. In the latter project, the gallery was driven till, by a peculiar instrument, it was ascertained that it had reached the walls of the place attacked, and then it was forced out right and left under their foundations, and supported by timber pillars. These were afterwards consumed by fire, and further shattered by powder, so that the support giving way, the walls fell into the gulf occasioned by the explosion.

These attempts were, however, often met by those who defended the fortifications, for the besieged were sometimes beforehand with their adversaries, and frequently met them face to face. Of this a remarkable instance occurred at the siege of a place called Melun in France, which was conducted by the Duke of Burgundy and our Henry V., in the year 1420. In that instance, the besiegers, who had driven up the mine close to the walls of the town, found, to their consternation and surprise, that their enemies had not been behindhand, and when the slight earthwork was broken through, and admitted an entrance into the town, the assailants perceived, with no little astonishment, their opponents ready to face them, and the king and the duke fought hand to hand with two of the inhabitants of the province of Dauphiny across the slight barrier that was left standing between the combatants.

Another of those terrible uses to which gunpowder is applied is the forcing open of the gates of fortified places, and a remarkable instance of the tremendous effect produced by it, was exhibited during the late war in India, when Afghanistan was overrun by the British forces. The long peace of Europe had thrown many of the military engineers out of employment, and

26

several had been taken into the service of the different poten-
tates and princes of India. Among such as had retained
some of these mercenaries, were the Ameers of Scinde, and when
the dispute with the British East India Company broke out,
they fortified Ghuznee, which was considered one of their
strongest fortresses. Every effort had been used to render the
place impregnable, and when their opponents approached, it
was fully believed by those in possession, that it was quite
strong enough to resist a siege of eight months, even if all the
powers of artillery were brought against it, and all the balls
fired that could be found in India.

The place was invested, and the ramparts presented a most
imposing appearance; but the troops were posted, and Lord
Keane, at that time in command of the British forces, determined to take the place by assault. About three hours before
daylight the men were placed, and Lieut. Durand, of the 71st
Highlanders, was commissioned to open the way for his com-
rades. The cannonade had been growing louder and louder for
a couple of hours; and every moment the peals of the musketry,
both from the walls and the assailants, became fiercer and
fiercer. The Afghans burnt blue lights to ascertain the position of their foes; and, in one of the intervals of darkness,
Durand advanced at the head of a party of men, each of whom
bore on his shoulders a leathern bag filled with gunpowder.
They succeeded in reaching the principal gate of the fortress
without being observed: within were the Afghan soldiers appointed to guard the entrance, each smoking his pipe with the
immovable gravity of Mahommedans, utterly unconscious of
the tremendous catastrophe that was instantly to hurry them
into eternity, and render all the precautions for the defence
of the town useless.

The bags were quickly attached to the gate; the train was
laid—the fuze was lighted; Durand and his men hurried to a
distance, and, in the next instant, there was a tremendous

27

explosion. The gate was scattered in fragments; the solid masonry of the walls, rent and torn, became a ruin; immense stones were hurled from their places; and all within the gate met with an instantaneous death. The way was opened; Colonel Denny, at the head of the forlorn hope, dashed over the ruins; and, notwithstanding the brave resistance of the defenders, the British flag soon waved over the ramparts.

Numerous examples of the powerful effects of gunpowder were given in that celebrated siege of Gibraltar, when it was assailed by the united forces of France and Spain, and defended by General Elliot. From its position at the entrance to the Mediterranean, Gibraltar has of late years been, as it will doubtless continue to be, a place of great political importance. It is connected on one side with the south-eastern coast of Spain; on its other sides the rock of the fortress bristling with cannon, and rough with the craggy protuberances by which its face is broken, towers in the highest part upwards of thirteen hundred feet above the waves that dash against its base, presenting one of the most formidable natural fortresses in the world.

Gibraltar had been taken by a combined English and Dutch fleet in 1704, and was confirmed as a British possession, in 1713, by the peace of Utrecht; but in 1779 it was assailed by the united forces of France and Spain, and the siege continued till the 2nd of February, 1788. The chief attack was made on the 13th September, 1782. On the part of the besiegers, besides stupendous batteries on the land side, mounting two hundred pieces of ordnance, there was an army of 40,000 men, under the command of the Duc de Crillon. In the bay lay the combined fleets of France and Spain, comprising forty-seven sail of the line, beside ten battering ships of powerful construction, that cost upwards of £50,000 each. From those the heaviest shells rebounded, but ultimately two of them were set on fire by red-hot shot, and the others were destroyed to prevent them from falling into the hands of the British commander. The rest of the fleet also suffered considerably; but the defenders escaped with very little loss. In this engagement 8300 rounds were fired by the garrison, more than half of which consisted of red-hot balls. During this memorable siege, which lasted upwards of three years, the entire expenditure of the garrison exceeded 200,000 rounds,—8000 barrels of powder being used. The expenditure of the enemy, enormous as this quantity is, must have been much greater; for they frequently fired, from their land-batteries, 4000 rounds in the short space of twenty-four hours. Terrific indeed must have been the spectacle as the immense fortress poured forth its tremendous volleys, and the squadron and land-batteries replied with a powerful cannonade. But all this waste of human life and of property was useless on the part of the assailants; for the place was successfully held, and Gibraltar still remains one of the principal strongholds of British power in Europe.

SAINT GEORGE'S HALL, GIBRALTAR.

29

During the progress of the siege, the fortifications were considerably strengthened, and numerous galleries were excavated in the solid rock, having port-holes at which heavy guns were mounted, which, keeping up an incessant fire, proved very efficacious in destroying the enemy's encampments on the land side. Communicating with the upper tier of these galleries are two grand excavations, known as Lord Cornwallis's and St. George's Halls. The latter, which is capable of holding several hundred men, has numerous pieces of ordnance pointed in various directions, ready to deal destruction on an approaching enemy.

In modern times one of the most striking examples of the power of gunpowder was shown in promoting the arts of peace. This was the experiment so boldly ventured upon by Mr. Cubitt, the civil engineer, who was employed to construct the South-Eastern Railway, and who, to avoid a tunnel of inconvenient length, determined to reduce the South Down Cliff, a portion of the chalk rock which girds the Kentish coast between Folkestone and Dover. The range of land between these two towns consists of a series of lofty hills, upraised by the chalk rock which extends from the middle of England to the centre of Poland, divided of course by the sea. It was desirable to avoid a long gallery, through which the trains would have had to pass, unless a durable sea-wall could be formed by which the carriages might proceed in open daylight. With characteristic force of intellect, Mr. Cubitt resolved to level this mighty barrier; and as the reduction of it, if accomplished by manual labour, would not only cost an immense expense, but would also occupy a great amount of time, the engineer determined to blow it up with gunpowder. Accordingly a gallery of small dimensions was opened in the rock from the western end; and at certain intervals chambers, or open spaces, were formed, in which large quantities of gunpowder were deposited. These chambers were then closed, only leaving small openings for the communication of fuzes, or ropes having within them a copper-wire which communicated with a little house on the surface, at a considerable distance from the spot where the catastrophe was to take place. These wires were attached, at the other extremity, to a galvanic battery, which, by the passage of electricity through them, would fire the gunpowder. Mr. Cubitt was assisted by Lieut. Jackson, of the Royal Engineers. On the day appointed for the operation a large assemblage was gathered on the Downs to witness the result of the experiment. There was nothing to be seen but the undulating surface of the country, and the multitude of gay spectators of this novel sight, with the sea stretching in repose beyond, a little hut in which the operators were engaged, and a small rope, which, at a short distance, seemed to be lost in the ground. The battery was charged, and, after a few seconds, a low rumbling noise was heard, apparently under foot—an almost imperceptible upraising occurred, and, within a few seconds afterwards, the whole of the immense mass of rock, weighing upwards of 500,000 tons, was cast forward, and lay ground and shattered on the edge of the Channel waters. It was calculated that upwards of eight months of labour, and £10,000 of expense, were saved by this bold experiment. It was a sight not to be seen once in a century; it was the carrying of a stubborn and ancient barrier by peaceable science—a turning of the elements of war into the channels of civilization.

It is almost needless to dwell on the several other offices of peace which gunpowder fulfils, but we must not omit to mention the great aid it renders in bringing to the surface of the earth those metals which constitute one of the great sources of this country's wealth. Few sights indeed are more striking than that of blasting rocks in a mine. When it is requisite to remove a large quantity of earth or stone, a perforation is formed in the side, at the end of which a chamber or

open place is made, and into this cavity the gunpowder is introduced; a fuze, so made as to allow the work. men to get to a safe distance before it ignites the powder, is then lighted, and in a few minutes the rock is torn from its bed, and the miners are enabled to proceed in the extraction of the mineral wealth which this explosion may bring to light.

Who it was that first invented gunpowder is unknown. It was for a long time believed that its properties were first discovered by Berthold Schwartz, a Prussian monk, but it is now generally agreed that it was used by the Chinese, many centuries before the Christian era, but only as an agent of peaceful arts, such as the levelling of roads, the reduction of hills, and the formation of canals, although some of their ancient pieces of ordnance seem adapted only for the use of gunpowder. Of its first application by them for the purpose of warfare we have no certain account; indeed, the earliest instance of its employment for the destruction of human life is found in the account of the battle of Crecy, fought with the French by our Edward III. in 1346.

Roger Bacon, the celebrated English natural philosopher, gives some obscure account of its composition in his treatise on Natural Magic, but, as just stated, to Berthold Schwartz the general knowledge of its real nature is traced. His discoveries were made known in 1336, ten years before cannon appeared in the field at Crecy.

Gunpowder is formed by a chemical mixture of nitre, charcoal, and sulphur, in different proportions. One would suppose, that as the objects to be attained are explosion, power, and rapidity of firing, or combustion, that the proportion of the several ingredients used would be the same for all purposes; but such is not the case. It is necessary, that whatever quantity of each ingredient be required, they must all be of the utmost purity. The charcoal is procured from burning alder, willow, or dogwood, and it is prepared, not in the usual way, but by consuming the woody fibre in iron retorts; the sulphur is of the volcanic kind, and is chiefly procured from Sicily, while the nitre is first fused to divest it of water, and afterwards wetted to enable it to mix with the other ingredients.

When these substances are in a fit state for mixing together, they are formed separately into pound powders, and then mixed in their proper proportions. They are afterwards sent to the powder-mill, which consists of two stones reared uprightly, and moving on a bed placed flat. On this bed the powder is deposited, and wetted sufficiently to enable the stones to act upon it without firing; but not so as to bring it into a state of paste. The stone runners are made to revolve over this mass until it is in a fit state to be sent to the *cooning house*, where it is cooned or grained. There it is pressed into a firm mass, and afterwards broken into small lumps and made to pass through sieves with small apertures, in which there is put a piece of wood called *lignum vitæ.*

The sieves are formed of parchment skins, which have round holes punched in them, and within the sieves the piece of *lignum vitæ* is made to revolve till it has forced all the powder through the apertures, and grains of several sizes are consequently formed. From these grains the dust caused by the rubbing is separated, and then the hard corners and edges of the particles left are taken off, by being run for some time in a reel, which is made to describe a circular motion by the aid of machinery. This process is called *glazing*, as it puts a slight gloss upon the powder, which is afterwards sent to a stove to be dried, care being taken to regulate the heat by a thermometer, that the sulphur may not be dissipated or driven off by the process. Only about forty or fifty pounds of this composition is worked at a time, as explosions occasionally occur from the upright stones coming in contact with the bed on which the powder is placed and on which they revolve.

The cause of the explosion of gunpowder is this: a spark falling on one particle heats it to the degree of ignition, then nitre is decomposed, and its oxygen being set free, immediately combines with the charcoal and sulphur, which are also made hot, and the combination produces heat enough to inflame the whole mass with such rapidity, as to cause it to force away any object before it with great power.

While on the subject of gunpowder, we may mention the apparently remarkable invention of a gentleman named Warner, a captain in the navy, who has lately offered to sell to the government the secret of his discovery for the benefit of the country, but demanded a large price as his reward. The value he placed upon his invention induced one of those noble-spirited and patriotic individuals who have risen through the exercise of their own faculties to station, influence, and wealth, of which the annals of the country contain so many examples, Mr. Joseph Soames, a shipowner, to present a vessel of his own, of about four hundred tons burden, to test the truth of Capt.

DESTRUCTION OF THE JOHN OF GAUNT.

Warner's assertions. That gentleman had declared that, without any communication with the vessel at all, he could in an instant blow the largest ship to atoms.

The experiment was made off the coast of Brighton; and, as the time approached, the shore was crowded with eager spectators, among whom were the government commissioners, and a large number of officers eminent in the military service of the country. Shortly before the time fixed, the John of Gaunt hove in sight, towed by a small steamer, while Capt. Warner, in another boat, was waiting to fulfil or disappoint the anxious multitudes on the cliff, who were observing his proceedings. The tow-rope was cast loose; and, at a signal from the shore, the inventor completed his design. The distance between Capt. Warner and the John of Gaunt might be from half to three-quarters of a mile; but within two or three minutes after the signal had been given, the fated vessel was seen to rise upon the surface of the sea, her decks were forced out, and, in the succeeding instant, her masts and rigging were

c 2

dishevelled, and she sank a ruin beneath the waters—a complete evidence how one puny hand, directed by reason and armed by science, can, in an instant, destroy the proudest vessel that may have braved unscathed the wildest storm.

Capt. Warner has also stated that, by his discovery, he is able to destroy ships even at five miles' distance, and with a variety of objects intervening; and a trial, at the expense of government, was made on the Marquis of Anglesea's estate in Wales. But it would seem that the invention is not yet complete, as the experiment in that instance failed.

Another equally efficacious, and indeed more powerful instrument of destruction than gunpowder, has of late been made known to the world by M. Schonbein, a professor of chemistry at Berlin. He found that by immersing the common flax cotton in equal quantities of nitric acid and sulphuric acid, and then washing and drying it, that an explosive power was obtained quite equal to that of gunpowder. It is stated in a report of the Parisian Academy of Sciences, that "if we are to believe the statements that have been made by persons of high respectability, the explosive cotton of M. Schonbein is a perfect substitute for gunpowder, possessing, weight for weight, much more strength than that article, and, at the same time, being free from the many serious objections which attend the manufacture of gunpowder. On the other hand, it does not appear that any of the specimens of other discoverers have given fully satisfactory results, that is to say, they are by no means of so destructive a property as the cotton of M. Schonbein. Many charges of illiberality have been brought against that gentleman for not making his process known, and endeavouring to make a good speculation of it for his own interest, under the protection of patents. We do not join in this outcry. If M. Schonbein, who is reported, we know not how truly, to have disposed of his patent right in England for £40,000, could make a million sterling of his different patents, we should not think him too highly rewarded, if it be true that his cotton is so much more powerful than that of his competitors, as his friends represent it to be. The man who invents the most rapid and the most effectual means of destruction, as regards war, is the greatest friend to the interests of humanity. Before gunpowder was invented war was a very favourite pastime of the rulers of nations, for it served to gratify their bad passions without presenting the chances of utter ruin to them. By risking a portion of the money derived from the labour of their subjects, and sacrificing a few hundred lives, they were able to play at the game of ambition; and, having always the hope of success before them, they had a constant excitement to violence and outrage. Nor did the pastime cease with the invention of gunpowder. The scale on which it was carried on was greater; but in a few years, when military tactics had been improved, and fire-arms had been made on surer principles, the game became too hot for the gamesters, and they were glad to retreat at length from the struggle of vain glory. The bow and arrow work of the ancients was nothing more than child's play to the fields of Austerlitz and Waterloo; and, when once a suspension of hostilities had taken place, governments began to reflect that the game was too costly. Thirty years of peace have served to give birth to better ideas; but there is every now and then an indication of a desire to involve nations in warfare. We are quite sure, however, that if any man could invent a means of destruction, by which two nations going to war with each other would see large armies destroyed, and immense treasure wasted, on both sides, in a single campaign, they would both hesitate at entering upon another. We repeat, therefore, that in this sense the greatest destroyer is the greatest philanthropist; and supposing what is said of M. Schonbein's invention to be true, we think that all governments will, in the event of differences, try all possible means of concession and conciliation before coming to a trial of strength in

37

which the strong as well as the comparatively weak must be such great losers."

No better result could have been desired, and as the world grows wiser the truth of these assertions will be not only readily recognised, but acted on. The governments of England and France have both declined to use the "gun-cotton," as it is called, instead of gunpowder, because it is alleged that it explodes with such a small degree of heat, that after a few discharges a musket would be so hot as to go off the moment the charge was put within the barrel.

The invention is not, however, quite so new in principle as was generally supposed, for at the same meeting of the academy to which we have alluded, M. Pelousi, one of the members, said, "Although M. Schonbein has not published the nature or mode of preparation of his cotton, it is evident that the properties which he assigns to it can only apply to xyloidine. M. Dumas, as well as myself, made this remark in the origin of the first communications of M. Schonbein. Reasoning on the hypothesis that the *poudre coton* is nothing else than xyloidine, I may be permitted to say a few words with respect to its history, and some of its properties. Xyloidine was discovered in 1833 by M. Braconnet, of Nancy. He prepared it by dissolving starch and some other organic substances in nitric acid, and precipitating these solutions in water. In a note inserted in the *Comptes rendûs de l' Academie des Sciences*, in 1833, I showed that the xyloidine resulted from the union of the elements of the nitric acid with those of starch, and explained, by this composition, the excessive combustibility of the substance produced. I ascertained—and this I think is a very important result in the history of the applications of xyloidine—that, instead of preparing it by dissolving the cellulose, it might be obtained with infinitely greater facility and economy by simply impregnating with concentrated nitric acid, paper, cotton, and hemp, and that these organic matters thus treated took fire at 180 degrees, and burnt almost without residuum, and with excessive energy; but I think it right to add, that I never for an instant had an idea of their use as a substitute for gunpowder. The merit of this application belongs entirely to M. Schonbein. Eight years ago, however, I prepared an inflammable paper by plunging it into concentrated nitric acid. After leaving it there for twenty minutes I washed it in a large quantity of water, and dried it in a gentle heat. I have recently tried this paper in a pistol, and with about three grains pierced a plank two centimetres in thickness (about three quarters of an inch) at a distance of twenty-five metres."

M. Otto, of Brunswick, Dr. Knapp, of Berlin, Mr. Taylor, of London, Mr. Phillips, of Brighton, and several other individuals connected with science, have produced similar results, not only from cotton, but from other vegetable products. The full effects of this discovery have not yet been ascertained, though its manufacture in this country is likely to be very extensive for both sporting and mining purposes. The history of explosive substances, so far as our present experience extends, may here be said to terminate. This review of them teaches us at least one truth, that mental exertion, especially when employed in scientific investigation, will always prove superior to brute force, no matter how skilfully directed.

CLOCKS.

THE measurement of Time must have been an art which the earliest of mankind were desirous of discovering. No accurate account of events could be transmitted to their posterity without it; and when human society began to take an orderly form, this division of time became the more necessary for the regular performance of social duties and labours.

The "lights in the firmament of the heaven" were not only to divide the day from the night, but were to be "for signs, and for seasons, and for days, and for years." The regulation of the "seasons" men beheld to be evidently dependent on the sun; and their periodical return began to be classed as comprising a "year."

The "day," or period between the apparent rising and setting of the sun, or, as inclusive of night, the period from sun-rise to sun-rise, would afford a ready means of enabling the first men to apply their rude science of numbers to the length of a year. The moon, by its succession of phases in twenty-eight days, afforded an easy reference for the subdivision of months; while the fourth of this period dictated the further subdivision of weeks, common to all the early nations.

Our own island-king, Alfred the Great, had no clock with which to measure out time, only the sun and shadow to divide the hours, both useless in the dull cloudy day and amid the darkness of night. To overcome this difficulty, and divide the night and day into twenty-four portions, he made wax candles, twelve inches in length, and each of these he marked at equal distances; and, although the time occupied in replacing and relighting them would scarcely serve to mark the lapse of minutes accurately, yet they were so equally made, that six of them, used in succession, with but little variation, burnt through the twenty-four hours. To guard against the casualties of winds and draughts, he enclosed these candles in thin white transparent horn, and this led to the invention of lanterns. It was several centuries after the death of this great king before clocks were discovered.

The division of the day into hours was fixed at the number twenty-four, from the earliest date of authentic history; but the means of determining the hours, with such further sub-divisions as would soon be found necessary, were at first very imperfect.

The *sun-dial* was in use among the earliest nations. Herodotus says that the Greeks borrowed it from the Baby-lonians. The art of Dialling, or Gnomonics, was, up to the end of the seventeenth century, considered a necessary part of a mathematical course; it will, now, be sufficient to explain familiarly the principles on which dials are constructed.

If a person were to place a staff in the ground, so as to point either vertically or otherwise, and to watch its shadow at the same hour, on different days at some intervals from each other, marking its direction at each day's observation, he would, in all probability, find that the direction of the shadow, the hour being always the same, varied from day to day. He might, however, find that the shadow was always in one direc-tion at the same hour, and this might happen in two different ways. First, he might by accident fix the staff in a direction parallel to that of the earth's axis, in which case the direction of the shadow would always be the same at the same hour, at all times of the year, and for every hour. Secondly, having fixed the staff in a position not parallel to the axis of the earth,

41

he might happen to choose that particular hour, or interval between two hours, at which the shadow of a staff in *that one direction* always points one way. But if, as is most likely, he were to fix the staff in a direction which is not that of the earth's axis; and if, as is again most likely, he were to choose any time of observation but one, the shadow would certainly point in different directions at different periods.

Now a sun-dial consists of two parts: the *gnomon* (represented by our supposed staffs), usually supplied by the edge of a plate of metal, always made parallel to the earth's axis, and therefore pointing towards the north; and the *dial*, which is another plate of metal, horizontal or not, on which are marked the directions of the shadow for the several hours, their halves and quarters, and sometimes smaller subdivisions.

The objections to a sun-dial are, that the shadow of the gnomon is not sufficiently well defined to give very accurate results, even for ordinary purposes; that refraction, which always makes the sun appear a little too high, throws the shadow a trifle towards noon at all times, that is, makes the time too fast in the morning, and too slow in the evening; and that a correction is always necessary in order to find mean or civil time. Even if the first objection could be got over, the corrections requisite for the two latter would prevent persons in general from making use of the instrument.

The *clepsydra*, or water-clock, which measured time on the principle of the common hour-glass, was in use among the Chaldeans and ancient Hindoos. Water was allowed to run out of the small orifice of a vessel, as sand falls from the common hour-glass, and by this means time was rudely measured. Sextus Empiricus tells us that the Chaldees used such a vessel for finding their astrological data, but remarks that the unequal flowing of the water, and the alterations of atmospheric temperature, rendered their calculations inaccurate. The truth of this observation may easily be verified by filling a glass cylinder with water, and slightly opening an orifice at one end held downwards; when it will be seen that the upper surface of the fluid will not descend equally in equal times. And again, if the cylinder be kept constantly full, it will discharge its own bulk of fluid in exactly one-half the time in which it will empty itself undisturbed. *Clepsydra* is a Greek word, and the use of this instrument in Athens is often indicated by Demosthenes in his pleadings. Such a meter of time was used in the courts of justice in Athens. In the third consulship of Pompey it was first adopted at Rome. Of what particular form the water-clocks of the East were, we have no means of judging; but from remaining Greek and Roman accounts we learn, that the water which fell drop by drop from the orifice of one vessel fell into another, floated a light body that marked the height of the water as it rose, and thus denoted what time had elapsed; but we further learn that these instruments required much care and regulation, in order to perform their end with the least approach to correctness.

Water-clocks, in modern times, have, however, been constructed with so much skill as to demand mention among the most ingenious contrivances. Dom Charles Vailly, a Benedictine monk, is said to have first improved the water-clock into a scientific instrument, about 1690; though others attribute the invention (which he first introduced in France) to Martinelli, an Italian. This instrument was made of tin, and consisted of a cylinder divided into several small cells, and suspended by a thread fixed to its axis, in a frame on which the hour-distances, found by trial, were marked. As the water flowed from one cell into the other, it very slowly changed the centre of gravity of the cylinder, and put it in motion, so as to indicate the time on the frame. By later improvements, an alarum, consisting of a bell and small wheels, was fixed to the top of the frame in which the cylinder was suspended, and afterwards, a dial-plate with a handle was also placed over the frame: the

43

advantages of our common clock were thus, in some measure, obtained.

The French historians describe a clock sent to Charlemagne in the year 807, by the famous Eastern Caliph, Haroun al Raschid, which was evidently furnished with some kind of wheel-work, although the moving power appears to have been produced by the fall of water. This clock was a rather wonderful affair, and excited a great deal of attention at the French court. In the dial of it were twelve small doors forming the divisions for the hours, each door opened at the hour marked by the index, and let out small brass balls, which, falling on a bell, struck the hours—a great novelty at that time. The doors continued open until the hour of twelve, when twelve figures representing knights on horseback came out and paraded round the dial plate.

Wheelwork was known and skilfully applied by Archimedes; but no description of any piece of mechanism resembling our clocks is found among the ancient Greeks. The term *horologe*, by which clocks only came to be denoted in process of time, was formerly applied indiscriminately to dials and clocks, so that nothing decisive, as to the era of invention, can be inferred from its use; nor is it possible to point out any individual who can with propriety be called the inventor of clocks. The first author who has introduced the term as applicable to a clock that struck the hours appears to be Dante, who was born in 1265, and died in 1321. In Italy, however, it would appear that striking clocks moved by weights were known in the latter part of the twelfth century. Our own country was in possession of these improved time-meters at rather a later period. In the 16th of Edward I., or 1288, a fine imposed on the Chief-Justice of the King's-Bench was applied to the purpose of furnishing a clock for the clock-house near Westminster Hall, which clock was to be heard by the courts of law. This clock was considered of such

44

consequence in the reign of Henry VI. (which commenced in 1422) that the king gave the keeping of it, with the appurtenances, to William Warby, dean of St. Stephen's, together with sixpence per day, to be received at the Exchequer. The clock at St. Mary's, at Oxford, was also furnished, in 1523, out of fines imposed on the students of the university. Mention is made in Rymer's "Fœdera" of protection being given by Edward III. to three Dutch horologers who were invited from Delft into England, in the year 1368 ; and we find in Chaucer, who was born in 1328, and died in 1400, the following lines:

> " Full sickerer was his crowing in his loge,
> As is a *clock*, or any abbey orloge."

In the year 1334 Giacomo Dondi erected at Padua his celebrated clock, which, besides the hour of the day, showed the course of the sun in the ecliptic, and the places of the planets. The celebrity which this clock acquired, tended greatly to advance this particular branch of mechanical art, and the author was dignified with the surname of Horologius.

About the middle of the fourteenth century, the famous Strasburg clock appears to have been erected in the cathedral church of that city. It was a most complicated piece of mechanism, the plate exhibiting a celestial globe, with the motions of the sun, moon, earth, and planets, and the various phases of the moon, together with a perpetual almanac on which the day of the month was pointed out by a statue ; the first quarter of the hour was struck by a child with an apple, the second by a youth with an arrow, the third by a man with the tip of his staff, and the last quarter by an old man with his crutch. The hour itself was struck on a bell by a figure representing an angel, who opened a door and saluted the Virgin Mary ; near to the first angel stood a second, who held an hour-glass, which he turned as soon as the hour had finished striking. In addition to these was the figure of a golden cock, which, on the arrival of every successive hour, flapped its

45

wings, stretched forth its neck, and crowed twice. Two hundred years after, this celebrated clock was almost entirely

THE STRASBURG CLOCK.

renewed, when great alterations in the original mechanism were made. At present we believe it has fallen quite into disuse. A clock with a similar complicated machinery, though differing considerably in its external performances, was erected somewhere about the year 1385 in the cathedral of Lyons.

The next important clock of which we have any description was regulated by a balance; it was the work of Henry de Wyck, a German mechanician of considerable ingenuity, and was placed in the tower of a palace of the Emperor Charles V. about the year 1364. This clock of De Wyck, and indeed all those made with a balance for the regulator, without any regulating spring, must have been very imperfect machines, yet our present clocks and watches are but improvements upon this rude beginning. At what period portable clocks were first made, is uncertain; there is, however, a story told of a gentlemen of the court of Louis XI. of France, which shows that the reduction of the time-piece to a portable compass had taken place towards the end of the fifteenth century. It appears that the courtier in question, after having lost a large amount of money at play, stole a clock belonging to the king, and hid it in his sleeve. The clock nevertheless continued its movements, and after a time gave notice of its place of concealment by striking the hour; this immediately discovered the theft, and the king, capricious in his kindness as well as in his cruelties, not only forgave the offender but actually made him a present of the clock. In the year 1544 the corporation of master clock-makers at Paris obtained from Francis I. a statute in their favour, forbidding any one who was not an admitted master to make clocks, watches, or alarms, *large* or *small*. Before portable clocks could be made, the substitution of the main-spring for a weight, as the moving power, must have taken place; and this may be considered a second era in horology, from which may be dated the application of the fusee; for these inventions completely altered the form and principles of horological machines.

The application of a pendulum to the clock, marked another era in their construction. Galileo and Huygens contended for the priority of applying the pendulum to clocks; but the honour really belongs to a London artist named Richard Harris, who invented and made a long-pendulum clock in 1641, seventeen years before the date at which Galileo describes himself to have made, or directed the making of one.

In 1617, Barlow, a London clock-maker, invented the repeating mechanism by which the hour last struck may be known by pulling a string; but a much more important addition to the improvements in clocks speedily followed, namely, the invention of the anchor escapement, which, like most others that have stood the test of time, belongs to the English. This was the work of Clement, a London clock-maker, in 1680.

It would be a matter of some difficulty to determine what artist first reduced the portable spring-clock to the dimensions of a watch to be worn in the pocket. The small clocks prior to the time of Huygens and Hooke were very imperfect machines; they did not even profess to subdivide the hours into minutes and seconds until the invention of the balance-spring, which is to the balance what gravity is to the pendulum, and its introduction has contributed as much to the improvement of watches as did that of the pendulum to clocks. The honour of this invention was warmly contested by the last-named individuals previous to 1658; but, so far as priority of publication is concerned, the honour is due to Hooke.

Towards the end of the last century a clock was constructed by a Genevan mechanic named Droz, capable of performing a variety of surprising movements, which were effected by the figures of a negro, a shepherd, and a dog. When the clock struck, the shepherd played six tunes on his flute, and the dog approached and fawned upon him. This clock was exhibited to the King of Spain, who was highly delighted with the ingenuity of the artist. The king, at the request of Droz, took an apple from the shepherd's basket, when the dog started up and barked so loud that the king's dog, which was in the same room, began to bark also. We are moreover informed, that the negro, on being asked what hour it was, answered the question in French, so that he could be understood by those present.

A common watch has for its moving power a main-spring, the variable force of which is equalized, or rendered uniform, by the introduction of the fusee—a very beautiful contrivance, which is, nevertheless, nothing more than a variable lever, upon which the main-spring acts through the medium of the chain. As the chain winds upon it, the distance from the centre of motion of the fusee to the semi-diameter of the chain which is in contact with it varies, in the proportion, that the distance of the centre of motion of the fusee to the semi-diameter of the chain, at that point where it leaves the fusee for the barrel, multiplied by the force of the main-spring acting on the chain at that time, shall be what mathematicians term a *constant quantity*—that is, it shall be the same whatever point of the fusee may be taken.

49

PRINTING.

Printing described by the monks as the work of magic.

FUST.   GUTTENBERG.   SCHOEFFER.
(The Inventors of Printing.)

Children returning from school with their horn-books.

F WE could call up before us the library of an English monastery in the olden time, we should see the monks seated at their desks, their ink, pens, brushes, gold, and colours before them: one busily employed in finishing some richly illuminated initial, another slowly adding letter to letter, and word to word, translating and copying the ancient manuscript before him as he progressed with his tedious task.   From day to day, and month to month, would he slowly proceed, forming those thick, angular, black-letter characters, with no cessation, saving to attend to his meals, his prayers, and his sleep, unless he paused now and then to erase some error he had made upon the parchment, as with his quaint old-fashioned knife he carefully obliterated the mistake, before he again proceeded with his labour. Greece and Rome were then the great marts for books, and many a journey did our ancient Saxon forefathers make to obtain those rare manuscripts, which they purchased at great cost, and, on their return to England, translated into the Saxon language, or merely multiplied copies from the Latin. So precious were manuscripts in those days, that an Anglo-Saxon bishop named Wilfred had the books of the four evangelists copied out in letters of gold upon purple parchment; and such value did he set upon the work when it was completed, that he kept it in a case of gold adorned with precious stones. Few men, excepting the monks, were capable of writing in those early times. We find Wilitred, the king of Kent, affixing to a charter the sign of the cross, and causing the scribe to add below, that it was on account of his ignorance of writing that he could not sign his name. Literature would have made greater progress among the Saxons than it did, had it not been for the ravages of the Danes. These brave but ignorant sea-kings were heathens, and they looked upon the Saxon Christians, who once worshipped Woden, and were idolaters like themselves, as renegadoes to the old religion, and thus considered that they were performing a pious duty by destroying their monasteries and libraries; for their ideas of heaven consisted in the belief that after death they should drink ale out of the skulls of their enemies, and feast off a bone whose bulk never diminished, however much they ate. Many valuable manuscripts, which had cost the Saxon monks years of labour to produce, were burned by the heathen invaders, or England would no doubt, but for these ravages, have possessed the most valuable histories of any country in Europe, since the commencement of Christianity. Many treasures that we lost for ever would have been made familiar to us in the present day, through the discovery of printing, but for these savage sea-kings.

It is a pleasing change to turn from the survey of a discovery like that of gunpowder, which only increases man's power of slaughter, to an inquiry into the origin of an invention so grand and important as that of printing. We leave the records of death and destruction, havoc and suffering, conquest and false glory, to enter on the path of an art which has already led to grand results in civilisation, and opened the door of science and wisdom, and that must better the condition of man. Every human invention sinks into inferiority when compared with the discovery of printing. The period of its birth, late as it was in human history, may, indeed, be styled the era of light—the commencement of true civilisation. Men built pyramids, reared obelisks and temples, dug canals, constructed aqueducts and bridges, and formed gigantic highways for the march of armies, thousands of years ago; but their civilisation, with a few bright exceptions, only amounted to an advance above barbarism compared with the progress society has made since the discovery of printing. Knowledge, it has been wisely said, is Power, and while the few possessed knowledge they too generally employed it only to rule over and keep down the many. And this condition of things must have continued but for the means of printing, which made knowledge universal.

The blessings which will be eventually derived from this discovery are certain; and yet the date of their complete accomplishment may be distant. We have already observed that man learns but slowly. The great consolation is, that now he possesses the means of learning, and also of recording all that he does learn, his discoveries cannot, again, be lost; his inventions can no more sink into oblivion. One discovery produces another—and printing renders it impossible that any valuable invention can fail to yield its full improvement for the human race. Languages much more philosophical in construction, and copious in expression, than any living tongues, were spoken and written in ancient times; but, so long as the thoughts they embodied were restricted to laborious methods of inscription, knowledge was, necessarily, confined to a few. The cheap and rapid multiplication of copies of thought was the grand end; and this the printing press, with all its improvements, and, above all, the application of steam-power to its original capacity, has secured.

Blocks, or pages of characters, were, beyond doubt, in use among the Chinese, centuries before the Christian era; and similar methods of producing copies of words were known among the monks in our own country, and other parts of Europe, at an early period, though they appear but rarely to have been made use of. But these modes of embodying thought, like the Oriental engraving on wood and stone, were too laborious and inconvenient to come into common practice to aid the general spread of knowledge. We almost wonder that the simple contrivance of moveable types did not present itself, until so late, to mankind; but its very simplicity, doubtless, as in the instance of other important discoveries, prevented the human mind from recognising its great utility, even if a glimpse of it were gained by the thinkers of ancient times.

The great merit of this discovery requires that we should give a clear account of the memorable person to whom the invention of printing owes its origin; while the individuals who were soon associated with him in the furtherance of the same eventful enterprize, deserve scarcely less enlarged notice at our hands.

In the early part of the fifteenth century, a young man, named *John Gænsfleisch*, who was born at the neighbouring village of Selgeloch, in the year 1397, went to reside at Mentz, or Mayence, with a family of the name of Guttenberg, whose appellation, from a not uncommon custom in primitive societies, he soon attained and ever afterwards bore. Whilst there he became implicated in one of the insurrections of the citizens against the nobility, which, during that part of the middle ages, were so frequent, and ultimately terminated in the establishment of the institutions which were the bases of the whole freedom of the commercial classes in Germany.

In this case, however, the movement appears to have been unsuccessful, for Gænsfleisch, or Guttenberg as he afterwards called himself, and is now called by others, was obliged to flee to Strasburg, where he had to look out for the means of a livelihood. Whether Strasburg was at that time a literary city or not, is not well known; but in all probability it was, as it is still a considerable mart for the sale of books. If it were, it is not unlikely that Guttenberg's mind might be turned to the making of books as a good mode of obtaining subsistence. While engaged in the slow and laborious occupation of taking off, page by page, the writings of others from the carved blocks, his enterprising intellect was directed to some means of hastening the process, and the germ of the notion broke upon him, the full development of which was to produce such glorious results. The supposition crossed him that if the several letters which are to be seen upon the block could be separated from each other, they might be put together again in different positions, and form other words; and thus there would be a power of endless combination with only a small stock of materials. How he elaborated the process we have no certain information, for his first object was, of course, to keep his discovery to himself.

After some years the anger of his persecutors was assuaged, and he returned to Mayence, where he met with a wealthy burgher, whom in all probability he had known in more prosperous times; and he then engaged in partnership with Herr Faust or Fust, and, together, they entered upon an undertaking to supersede the laborious occupation of the manuscript-writer. Between them—for to which the honour is due is not clearly explained—they hit upon the expedient of casting their types in metal, which, being a more durable substance, was likely to increase and perpetuate their profits. Fust had at this time a young man in his employment whose name was Peter Schoeffer, a native of Hesse Darmstadt, who entered warmly into their designs, and who suggested the idea of stamping the forms of the letters in lead or other soft substance, so that they could renew their characters as they liked. This they succeeded in accomplishing; and thus the whole of the initiatory process of printing was fully obtained. The principle of the screw press had long been known, for it was just the time when the learning and scientific principles of the ancients were beginning to be revived. Here the whole principle of printing was developed. Yet years were necessary to bring the art, even in its primitive state, into actual operation. From the best accounts it would appear that the connection between Guttenberg and Fust commenced shortly after the year 1440; but their labours were not productive till nearly ten years after that date.

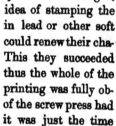

It has been stated that the letters were, in the first instance, made of wood, but it was quickly perceived that this was a substance quite unfitted for long service, and Schoeffer being ardently desirous of promoting the design of Fust, discovered the method of forming the letters at the bottom of a sort of case or mould called a matrix. He privately cut the whole alphabet, and when he showed his master the result of his labours and ingenuity, Fust was so delighted that he promised to give him his only daughter, Christina, in marriage—a promise which he soon afterwards fulfilled. The types first cast are supposed to have been of lead, but afterwards, by the infusion of antimony, the metal was made sufficiently hard to bear the work to which it was subjected.

The harmony between the partners appears to have been interrupted soon after Schoeffer entered the business, and in 1458 Guttenberg was obliged to retire from the concern, and he shortly afterwards left Mayence for a number of years—not, however, until he had completed several works of importance, and among others an edition of the Bible, now known as the Mazarine Bible, which met with a ready and extensive sale. A curious story is told, and certainly with the air of much veracity about it, to the effect that the copies of the Scriptures printed by Guttenberg and his companions, were produced so quickly, that none but the devil was considered competent to make them. Certain it is that when these copies were circulated in Paris, that they were eagerly bought up by the Roman Catholic authorities, and that thus fresh funds were supplied for the production of new editions.

A statue of Guttenberg, by the celebrated sculptor Thorwalsden, was erected at Mayence on the 14th of August, 1837, and deputations from all the great cities of Europe attended the ceremony, to do honour and homage to the inventor of printing. This statue of the man who had won for his city the gratitude of the world was exposed to view amid such joyful demonstrations of popular feeling as have been wont only to greet the return of some mighty conqueror.

The knowledge of the art of printing was first generally spread by the dispersion of the men in the employment of its three originators, which occurred in consequence of the storming of Mayence by the Archbishop Adolphus of Nassau, in 1462. In three years afterwards it was practised at Subiaco, in Italy; and was followed at Paris in 1469; it was introduced at Westminster, by Caxton, in 1474; and had spread as far as Barcelona, in Spain, by the year after; and in little more than half a century after that, it had become common all over Europe.

From that time down to the close of the last century there appears to have been no alteration in the mode of proceeding—the improvements consisting in the gradual increase in the size and the power of the press, and the greater beauty and variety of the types.

It would appear from the device of Badins Ascensius, an eminent printer of Paris and Lyons at the beginning of the fifteenth century, as well as from that of Anthony Scholoker (an Englishman, notwithstanding his name), at Ipswich, that the matrices and punches then used were much in the same form as at the present time. For a long period the printers were their own typefounders; but when the business began to spread rapidly, the casting of the letters became a separate business. The earliest authentic record of this change, which contributed so materially to the improvement of the art, is found in a decree of the Star Chamber, dated the 11th of July, 1637. This decree was issued for the suppression of publications issued by the Puritans and those joined with them in opposition to the Government, and who, it was believed, had established secret printing-offices for that purpose. By that decree it was ordained that there should only be four letterfounders throughout the kingdom; and that when any vacancy occurred in that number, by death or otherwise, that it should only be filled up under the orders and with the sanction of the archbishop of Canterbury—the primacy being at that time held by Laud, bishop of London, and six other commissioners. The decree also imposed the most stringent regulations on the taking of apprentices and the employment of journeymen.

Although the Commonwealth was established under the supposition that it was to increase and confirm the liberty of the subject, many of the arbitrary and unconstitutional regulations of the Star Chamber remained in force (even when the Court itself had been abolished), and among others the restraint of the typefounder. The restrictions, therefore, remained in force and were enacted into a law in the second year after the assumption of power by Charles II., and were continued for limited periods two years afterwards. They were again renewed for seven years in 1685, shortly after the accession of his brother James II.; but finally expired at the end of that term in 1693, when the Bill of Rights had finally established and confirmed the Great Charter of Henry III.

For the introduction of printing into England we are indebted to William Caxton, and his successor Wynkin de Worde, who established for themselves a high reputation both as printers and letterfounders. Caxton, who, in many respects, was a very remarkable person, and a man of eminent ability, was, according to his own account, born in the Weald of Kent, about the year 1412; and in his eighteenth year was apprenticed to Master Robert Large, a mercer in London of very considerable eminence, who afterwards became both sheriff and lord mayor of the City. By virtue of his indentures Caxton became a freeman of the Mercers' Company; and that his conduct was good, is shown by the fact that his master, at his death, left him a legacy of twenty marks as a testimony of respect. That Caxton had acquired reputation also as a man

of business is evident, for shortly after this time we find him travelling in what were called the Low Countries, either as an agent or on his own account. There he obtained both experience and respect, for in 1464 he was joined in a commission with Robert Whitehill to consolidate or make a commercial treaty between Philip, the then duke of Burgundy, and our King Edward IV., and in this commission they were styled ambassadors and special deputies. In 1469, during a period of comparative leisure, he began a translation of Raoul le Fevre's French History of Troy, and finished it about three years afterwards, having in the meantime entered into the service of Margaret, duchess of Burgundy, who assisted him with critiques upon his English, and liberally rewarded him on the conclusion of his book.

It was his leisure that in all probability gave him his taste for literature, and brought him into contact with the printers, whose profession was at that time not only novel, but also lucrative and highly honourable. How he acquired a knowledge of the art is not known, but, according to the account of de Worde, he was printing his first work at Cologne in 1470. He had not, evidently, at that time, seen the beautiful productions of the Parisian and Venetian presses; and his own types were consequently cut in some part of Flanders and Brabant. In 1474 he returned to England, and set up his press in the Almonry at Westminster, then a rural spot, with a sufficient

population to render it cheerful. The house he occupied, which is represented in the above woodcut, fell to the ground we believe in the early part of 1847. Caxton's second office was in King Street, and Wynkin de Worde, after his death, removed it to the present great mart of printing in the neighbourhood of Fleet Street.

Caxton's first work in the opinion of some was "The

Game of Chesse ;" but, according to others, it was the original of Raoul's History ; his third work was his own translation of this history, and his second the Oration on Russell being created a Knight of the Garter. He combined in himself the three separate callings of author, printer, and publisher, and by his own translations from the French, and the translations which he caused to be made, contributed greatly to stimulate the literature of his native country. He appears to have made use of five distinct founts of type. According to Rowe Mores, his first was what was called *Secretary*. He had also other founts, one of about *English* face, and three others of *Great Primer*, one rudely cut in 1474, and another much better, and a third, a vast improvement on the other two, cut in 1482 ; another fount of *Double Pica*, cut in 1490, and another of the body of *Long Primer*, which he used shortly afterwards. At this time all the books were printed in the old black letter, as it was called—that is, an imitation of the mode of writing used by the monks. Towards the middle of the sixteenth century the style of type now used to express an emphatic word was introduced by Aldus, and was called, from the place of its origin, *Italic*. The greater plainness of the Roman characters being soon perceived, they subsequently, but gradually, superseded all other kinds of type for book-work, except in Germany.

Although the efforts of Caxton and Wynkin de Worde had firmly established the art of printing in this country, still typefounding remained in a depressed state for many years afterwards, and England was for a long time supplied with its letter from the Continent. Indeed the art was at so low a point that the London printers only used the types imported from the Dutch foundries in superior works. But a change was to come over this state of things, and William Caslon, the founder of a house which yet exists, and which is still represented by one of the same name and family, as honourable and as high-minded a man as ever graced

60

commercial life, has the merit of removing this disgrace from his country. Caslon, in the early part of the last century, was employed in engraving ornaments and cutting letters for the use of bookbinders; but having finished some remarkably neat specimens of his art in the latter branch, he was engaged by the Society for the Promotion of Christian Knowledge in 1720 to cut a set of punches for an Arabic fount. In this, and his succeeding efforts, he was prompted and assisted by William Bowyer, who was himself a man of learning and a printer, and the son of a printer, and therefore quite competent to understand and appreciate the abilities of the man to whom he lent his aid. The result was that the Caslon Foundry not only obtained a pre-eminence for the British types, and put an end to the demand for those from abroad, but occasioned considerable call for the article from the best offices on the Continent. Nor has the firm which he originated lost any of its credit for business or artistical qualities.

The next name eminently deserving of celebrity in this line is that of John Baskerville, of Birmingham. Baskerville was himself a striking instance of the force of ingenuity and ability overcoming the opposition of circumstances. He was born at Wolverly, in Worcestershire, in 1706, and had early to find a living for himself. When only twenty years of age he was keeping a school at Birmingham, and soon afterwards became connected with the japanning business at that place, by which he realised a considerable property. But his taste for literature induced him to turn his attention to the improvement and perfection of the art of printing, yet still retaining his old concern.

Caslon had made considerable improvement upon the Dutch types before Baskerville's attempts at typefounding; but with that improvement the latter was not satisfied, and zealously set himself to carry it further, and most eminently succeeded— not however, it is stated, until after he spent upwards of £600 before he could get a single letter to please him, and several thousands before he realised any profit from the pursuit. His types, however, ultimately were of great beauty; and at his death, in 1775, were sold by his widow to a literary society at Paris, and were used in printing some of the best editions of their first classics. He doubtless laid the foundation for that beautiful style of letter which has of late years so greatly improved our own castings.

The Glasgow foundries, as well as those of Edinburgh, have always stood in high estimation. Typefounding was commenced at Glasgow in 1718, by James Duncan, whose foundry afterwards came into the hands of Mr. Alexander Wilson, a gentleman of great shrewdness, ability, energy, and ultimately of capital, and whose descendants at the present day continue to exhibit the same excellent qualities as he who laid the foundation of their present property and position. Another foundry was established by Dr. Fry, who got together the most complete set of founts for the Oriental languages that probably ever existed, and the business has been continued most worthily by his successor, Mr. Thorowgood, and his partner, Mr. Besley, followed *passibus equis* by the Messrs. Figgins, and Messrs. Stephenson, Blake, and Company, of Sheffield—all of those which we have enumerated classing, for the extent of their means and material, and for the beauty of their productions, in the first order of their profession.

Abroad the advancement of the art has been equally attended to, and very extensive foundries exist both in Germany and France as well as in Italy—the Propaganda in the last named country possessing one of the most complete establishments in the world. That, however, does not exceed in extent the foundry of Brieskopf, which is said to contain punches for not less than four hundred alphabets. Nor is it equal to that of Didot, in Paris, where the most minute and beautiful specimens of ordinary typography have been produced that ever were seen in the world—some of them, it is said, even requiring a magnifying glass to read them, the press-work being equally admirable with the beauty of the letters which compose the words. In the latter respect, however, especially in the production of those illustrated works which require the combination of artistical science and skill—and of which this little volume may serve as a humble example—English printers infinitely surpass all others.

Of the convenient form, and gradual improvement, of the *cases* in which the letters are contained, it is needless to say anything. As time proceeded, the best mode developed itself, and the order in which the letter is placed or *laid* differs even at present in some offices, although one plan is generally observed.

There are two *cases*, *upper* and *lower*, the *upper* for capital and small capital letters, the *lower* for small letters, divided into compartments for each, those most frequently in use being largest and nearest the compositor's hand. The compositor, having placed his *copy* on the upper case in front of him, takes in his left hand his *composing stick*, a small iron frame with slider and screw, which is capable of being adjusted to any required length of line, and with the forefinger and thumb of the right hand he picks up the types forming the words of his copy, and receives them with the thumb of the left in the stick, feeling that the *nick*, which is on the under side of each type, is uppermost as he drops it into its place. Between words are inserted *spaces*, which being lower than the letters do not produce an impression on the paper, and, varying in thickness, allow each line to be spaced out to a uniform width. All the letters are separate pieces of metal, fitting closely to each other; and, in a page such as this, there are upwards of 2,000 distinct pieces, each of which the compositor has to pick up separately, his wages being regulated by the number of thousands he sets up.

It is nevertheless requisite to remark that attempts have lately been made to supersede to a very great extent the manual labour of the compositor, in the arrangement of the letters, by two machines, which are acted on in the same way as the keys of a piano-forte are touched. The letters of each kind are arranged in different compartments, and one of each drops through, at each touch, as the key opens a valve at the bottom of the receptacle. These machines—the invention of Messrs. Young and Delcambre—are exceedingly ingenious; but peculiar skill and a long education is required before they can be brought into effective play, and either from the indisposition of men to quit their old habits, or from the want of capital, on the part of the proprietors, to submit their inventions to the principals of establishments in an effective state, they have received very scanty encouragement in any department of the business.

If, however, it has hitherto proved unprofitable to adapt machinery to the process of arranging the types, such has not been the case with regard to the impressions to be taken from them. Until towards the close of the last century, but little improvement had been made in the form of the old wooden printing press, except, as has been stated, in enlarging the size and increasing the power of the screw. But, at the period alluded to, Earl Stanhope, a nobleman of great ingenuity, who was himself an amateur printer, and exceedingly desirous of improving the art, invented, and, with the assistance of Mr. Walker, a skilful machinist, brought to perfection, an iron press in which the power, instead of being derived from the screw, was derived from a bent lever that impressed the platten or iron plate upon the paper, which is brought down on the surface of the types. The peculiar property of this press is, that when the platten first moves

ANCIENT WOODEN PRINTING PRESS, 1498.

downward, its motion is rapid, while, when the power is about to be applied, it is slow, so that the greatest amount of force is concentrated just at the time when it can be of the greatest effect. This press of Lord Stanhope's was followed by several others, for which patents were taken out; all of very ingenious construction, and which came into very general use. The most powerful of those was one called the Columbian press, invented by an American named Clymer; and the quickest in its action was the Albion press, invented by Mr. Cope of Finsbury, and greatly improved by his successor, Mr. Hopkinson. The power in both these is obtained from the effect of levers alone.

A press called the Ruthven press was much used when first brought out. Its peculiarity consists in the bed on which the type is placed being stationary, while the platten producing the impression is drawn over by the hand. It has very con-

HOPKINSON'S IMPROVED ALBION PRESS.

siderable power, but from the bar being pressed down by the
left hand is very laborious to the pressman, and owing to the
confined position of the works preventing their being oiled or
cleaned with facility it is now almost entirely disused ; and
those now more generally adopted for manual printing are on
the principles of Clymer and Hopkinson.

Of the various modes adopted for the execution of those
beautiful works in which several colours are used for embellish-
ment, we have not space, within the limits here assigned, to
speak. The examples which have already. issued from the
type press show to what an extent this beautiful art has been
carried. Want of room also prevents us from dwelling upon
the equally beautiful art of printing from wood engravings,
in which the lines, instead of being sunk beneath the surface,
as in copper plates, are left raised, the other portions of the
surface being cleared away.

To enter fully into these processes, as well as the departments of lithography and copperplate printing, would require

a volume. Let us, however; turn to the crowning discovery, the application of the *Steam Engine*, which makes the printing press, in one sense, a voluntary machine, and brings by its aid the productions of the noblest genius within the reach of the myriads whose means little more than suffice for the necessaries of life. This was accomplished by the invention of the *Printing Machine*, by which cylindrical pressure is applied in lieu of the flat, or platten, impression obtained by the common press.

Before, however, stating the circumstances of the application of steam power to printing, we should notice an invention, without which we may almost venture to say steam-machine printing could never have been generally adopted. This is an improvement for inking the types by means of composition rollers. Printing ink consists chiefly of lamp-black and varnish, with some other constituents to increase the brilliancy of the colour, and to keep the principal substances in coherence with each other. Formerly the ink was laid upon a flat surface by a little triangular piece of iron, with a handle to it, called a slice. A small portion of it was then taken and brayed out with a sort of wooden mallet as evenly as possible. The workmen employed to put the ink upon the *forme* (or a quantity of types which are arranged in their several pages in certain positions on the bed of the press, where they are to give their impression to the paper) held in each hand a wooden stock, in the shape of a stone-mason's hammer, which was hollowed out on its lower surface. That hollow was stuffed with wool, until there was a convex surface formed, and over this there was stretched a piece of untanned sheepskin, so as to be perfectly tight, even, and smooth. These are technically called *balls;* and the great art of keeping them fit for service consisted in retaining the *pelts* or sheepskin in a certain state of moisture and softness, so that they would receive the ink equally all over. The pressman, having taken a small portion of this ink on one of the balls, worked it against the other spirally, and occasionally dabbing the balls together until the ink was very evenly

spread or *distributed* over them both. With these he then dabbed the forme, keeping them constantly twirling round in his hands, when not absolutely touching the face of the types, until at length the whole of the letters were equally and sufficiently covered. This process required great nicety, and was moreover very laborious, while considerable trouble and attention were necessary to keep the balls in proper working order. All was at length obviated by the discovery of Mr. Foster, who, by the intermixture of glue, treacle, tar, and isinglass, formed a composition which retained all the requisite qualities of softness, elasticity, and readiness to receive and impart the ink, and which could, moreover, be made to adhere round a wooden

roller. It completely obviated a most unpleasant and unprofitable part of the art, and has proved of apparently indispensable value in machine printing. These rollers have of late years been immensely improved by the ingenuity of the Messrs. Harrilds, of Great Distaff Lane, in the city of London, and an inspection of the apparatus, which they possess for making composition balls and rollers, will amply gratify any one who has a taste for the useful arts.

But, to return to the Printing Machine. The want of some means to meet the increasing demand for books and newspapers had long been felt, and as early as 1790, before even Lord Stanhope's press had been brought into use, Mr. W. Nicholson had taken out a patent for two machines, the one somewhat resembling in outward form the common hand presses of that time, but the other very similar to the machines now in general use. In both these machines, which he describes as being applicable to printing books, paper-hangings, calico, linen, silk, &c., he proposes to make use of *cylindrical* instead of *surface* pressure, and to derive his motive power from wind, water, *steam*, or animal strength. Although Mr. Nicholson published the details of his process with drawings of the requisite machines, he was not successful in getting his invention generally adopted by the trade. His numerous pursuits, combined with the sudden death of his patron Lord Camelford, in all probability prevented his bestowing that constant application so necessary to establishing a new invention. Some years afterwards, one Herr König, a German, who had been unable to obtain any support on the Continent, came over to this country with the idea of applying *steam*, as the moving power, to *common presses*, which by his plan should acquire accelerated speed, and at the same time dispense with the employment of the man who inks the types. Three enterprising printers, Messrs. Bensley, sen., R. Taylor, and G. Woodfall, liberally supplied the necessary capital to the ingenious foreigner. After spending several years in fruitless experiments to reduce his ideas to practice, König abandoned this scheme and turned his attention to cylindrical machine printing, the practicability of which, as we have before stated, Mr. Nicholson had demonstrated in 1790. Two or three years of renewed exertion passed away, and finally a small machine was produced by König, capable of working 1,000 impressions per hour, and requiring only the superintendence of two boys. This machine was set to work in April, 1811, and 3,000 copies of part of the " New Annual Register " was printed by this means. This machine proving successful, it was considered practicable so to extend its principles and capabilities as to print a newspaper. As the accomplishment of this object was highly desirable, the late Mr. Walters, proprietor of the "Times" newspaper, was shown the machine already erected, and also made acquainted with the contemplated improvements. The result was, that an agreement was entered into with that gentleman, for the erection of two larger machines, for printing his journal, which at once brought the merits of the invention into general notice. On the 28th of November, 1814, the readers of the "Times" newspaper were informed that they were, for the first time, perusing a paper printed by the application of steam power.

These machines were necessarily of a very complicated construction, and it may suffice to say that each consisted of a number of cylinders, which so revolved as to carry the sheets of paper, through the agency of a number of tapes and wheels, placed between them and the types on the surface of the table, which constantly moved backwards and forwards, receiving in turn the ink from the inking rollers, and impressing its form on the paper subjected to its influence. Each of these machines was only capable of printing one side of the newspaper, and the sheets thus half printed by the one were *perfected*, as it is technically termed, by the other. The performance of these machines was in every way satisfactory, so far as they went; but they were shortly afterwards greatly improved upon, at least in the simplicity of their construction, by Messrs. Applegarth and Cowper, who were, at the time of König's invention, at the head of one of the most considerable typographical establishments in the metropolis. Their principle was much the same as that of König's, but they did away with many of the intricate parts, removing at one stroke *forty* superfluous wheels, and making the machine altogether more simple, available, and permanent. These gentlemen, having patented their improvements, erected a new machine for the "Times," which cost the proprietor of that newspaper £3,000.

The next improvement was the construction of a *perfecting machine* by König, for Messrs. Bensley, which delivered the sheet of paper printed on both sides. This double, or perfecting machine, threw off from 800 to 900 sheets per hour, worked on both sides; while the single, or non-perfecting machine, delivered in the same space of time from 1,300 to 1,400 sheets printed only on one side.

COWPER'S DOUBLE CYLINDER MACHINE.

Messrs. Donkin and Bacon in 1818 obtained a patent for a most ingenious but complex machine, which claims the merit of being the first to print with the types arranged upon a horizontally revolving cylinder, instead of being placed on a fixed table as in other machines. Although the fundamental principle of this invention was found objectionable, one great point was gained, namely, the introduction of the composition inking rollers, which were first applied to this machine, and immediately superseded those covered with leather which were used by König.

After this came Mr. Napier, one of that distinguished family whose scientific abilities and attainments we have before had to notice, and which have secured to them a reputation wide as the extent of civilization. He still further simplified

71

the printing machine, and secured the more easy, certain, and excellent working of the formes.

Some years after the erection of Cowper and Applegarth's machine at the "Times" office, the increased circulation of the "leading journal" rendered more rapid means of printing its daily number highly necessary. This demand was satisfied by Mr. Augustus Applegarth, who skilfully and ingeniously combined in one leviathan machine four of the single or non-perfecting machines, all being simultaneously driven by steam. In this machine, which prints the "Times" at the present day (May, 1848), there are four places at which to feed it with paper, four printing cylinders, and four places at which the sheets are delivered when printed; the combined action of these four auxiliaries producing from 4,350 to 4,500 sheets per hour, printed on one side.

It may be observed as a somewhat remarkable fact that the periodical inefficiency of the "Times" printing machines, to supply its almost incredible circulation with sufficient promptitude, is the cause of every progressive step in the improvement of printing machinery. At the time we write the machine just described, which for years has been considered a typographical wonder, is found incompetent to supply the increased demand for the "Times" newspaper. We understand Mr. Applegarth is again engaged in constructing a new machine to print from 8,000 to 10,000 sheets per hour. The principle totally differs from all the machines we have been describing, inasmuch as the types are piled up one upon another, laterally, round a large cylinder which revolves in a perpendicular position instead of in an horizontal one, as was the case with Donkin and Bacon's machine. The sheets of paper are supplied edgeways in an upright position, something like what you would adopt to pass sideways through a tall narrow entrance; while in the ordinary machines, to carry out the common-place simile we have adopted, the sheets are supplied horizontally, as you would pass on your stomach through an aperture which, from its diminutive height, is only capable of admitting you in a recumbent position.

It is however greatly doubted, by skilful engineers, whether the principle of Mr. Applegarth's new machine will be found to work with sufficient perfection when thoroughly tested.

In concluding this article, we feel much pleasure in recording Mr. Little's invention of the Double Action Printing Machine, for working daily newspapers at a speed varying from 10,000 to 12,000 copies per hour, while the average rate of production of the Four Cylinder Fast Machines at present in use is not more than 4,500 per hour.

The principle of the Double Action Machine being the solution of a problem which the most scientific machinists had hitherto considered impossible, our young readers would only be puzzled were we to present them with too minute a description of its construction; we shall therefore confine ourselves to explaining its advantages, by comparing it with one of the present Fast Machines, working with four cylinders, two of which constantly revolve in one direction, while the remaining two move unceasingly in an opposite direction. With this machine only two sheets of paper can receive an impression from the forme of type with each passage of the table on which the type is placed. The reason of this is, the cylinders which cause the impression must always travel in the same direction as the table. Thus, while two of the cylinders are occupied in giving impressions, the other two are waiting the return of the table, so that the machine produces two printed sheets with every forward, and two with every backward motion of the type, making four in all. Now the Double Action Machine works with eight cylinders, six of which have a reversing motion, by which they print first forwards and then backwards. This machine produces *seven* printed sheets with every passage of the table on which the forme of type is placed, just the same as in the Four Cylinder

Machine. If our young friends be sufficiently interested in the machine we are describing, they will naturally wonder why the *eight* cylinders only produce *seven* sheets. The reason is this: in consequence of six of the cylinders having a reversing motion, by which they print first forwards and then backwards, it is necessary that the two end cylinders (the 1st and the 8th) should work slower, while the reversing of the other six takes place; thus it is explained why the end cylinders ,only print one sheet each, while the remaining six produce two sheets each, from every revolution of the table.

Now while in the Four Cylinder Machine only half the cylinders are working, in the Double Action Machine seven out of eight are continually occupied in printing, and another great advantage possessed by the latter machine is the great saving effected in the distance the forme of type has to travel. This, combined with the constant working of seven cylinders, causes the machine, as we have before stated, to produce from 10,000 to 12,000 newspapers per hour, while the Four Cylinder Machines print only 4,500 in the same space of time.

Before the invention of the Printing Machine, the newspaper offices, in order to supply the number of copies required for daily publication, were compelled to *set up* or compose the types twice, and on extraordinary occasions even three and four times over. In those days the newspapers were necessarily much smaller than at the present time, and were worked by hand presses, the types being inked with the sheepskin balls already described. The speed at which the men were compelled to work required such great exertion that the stoutest constitutions, after a few years' time, fell sacrifices to such laborious occupation. Hence, beyond the advantage of rapidly producing the daily papers, we may regard the invention of the Printing Machine as highly beneficial to humanity.

To attempt to describe the several portions of the Printing Machine would be useless, as it will be by far the best understood by the engraving which is given at page 71. Other plans have been adopted, and several flat surface machines, which communicate the impression by a platten like the ordinary press, and are admirably adapted for fine book-work, are now in use. Their motion is similar to that of the hand press, and the work produced by them almost equals that from the hand press in excellence.

NAPIER'S PLATTEN MACHINE.

The most recently constructed platten machine is that of Messrs. Napier & Son, in which the inking apparatus is brought to very great perfection. A considerable portion of the " Boy's Own Library " is printed by this machine.

Another highly important invention connected with the art of typography is the process of *Stereotyping*, by which all the letters, forming a page of type, are cast in one piece or plate of type-metal about the eighth of an inch thick.

This process was first practised by William Ged, of Edinburgh, in the year 1725, who, after much perseverance, formed an arrangement with the University of Cambridge for casting their Bibles and Prayer-Books, thereby saving the necessity of employing a large quantity of type; but the plan received so much opposition from the workmen, in making errors and injuring the plates, that it was discontinued, and the stereotypes ultimately melted down at the Caslon Foundry.

The merits of the invention were, however, eventually recognised, and its adoption has become almost universal. We will now endeavour to explain the process. The moveable types of two or four pages, according to their size, are first slightly oiled over with a brush, and then burnt plaster of Paris (termed gypsum), mixed with water to the consistency of cream, is poured upon the pages, which are surrounded by narrow slips of wood, or metal, forming a wall just sufficiently high to retain enough of the plaster mixture to produce a matrix, or mould. This matrix is left until the greater portion of the moisture becomes evaporated. It is then lifted from the type and is put into an oven to dry, or rather bake out all the remaining moisture. It is next secured in a flat dipping-pan, surrounded by an iron frame which regulates the thickness of the stereotype plate, and the pan being covered is immersed in a cauldron of melted metal, where it remains sufficiently long for the metal thoroughly to insinuate itself into every part of the matrix. The dipping-pan being removed from the cauldron, sufficient time is allowed for the metal to *set*. It is finally cooled by being plunged into cold water, and the superfluous metal is sawn from the stereotype plate by a circular saw. The back of the plate thus produced is turned in a lathe to a certain guage, which regulates all the plates forming the pages of a book to one uniform thickness.

When stereotype plates are printed they are fixed upon wooden or metal stands of such thickness that when the plate is added the two combined become exactly the same height as the regular printing types. Stereotype plates are adapted for working both by hand presses and machines.

THE THERMOMETER.

HE origin of the Thermometer, like that of the mariner's compass, remains in obscurity. We only know that the idea of measuring the degree of heat, which the atmosphere at different periods presents, was first conceived in Italy, that country which, during the latter portion of the middle ages, was distinguished by the attainments and discoveries of its scientific men.

In the year 1626, there was a book published entitled, "Commentaries on the Works of Avicenna," by a physician, named Santoria, who resided at Padua; and in this work he claims the honour of having invented the thermometer. Cornelius Drebble, of Alkmaar in Holland, makes the same claim, and after carefully examining the evidence, it appears, that although Santoria was the first to point out the use of this instrument, Drebble had also discovered and made its properties known before he heard anything of the invention of the Italian physician.

For some time after the invention of the thermometer, it was chiefly used for ascertaining the changes of temperature alone, and the instrument was of the simplest description. A glass tube was formed with a ball at one end; the other end was open, and inserted in a vessel partly filled with mercury or coloured spirit—generally the latter. Previous to this the air inside the instrument was heated by a lamp, so that when the temperature of the atmosphere was increased, it caused the air within the ball and the tube to be rarified. As this expanded and occupied more space, it pressed down the spirit; and on the contrary, when the temperature was reduced, its pressure upon the surface of the spirit decreased, and the latter was forced higher up the tube, as the quantity of air within became contracted in bulk. A scale was then fixed alongside the tube, divided into certain degrees, so that the several changes could be measured as correctly as might be expected from the simplicity of the contrivance.

Such an invention was not long before it attracted notice; and after a few years the celebrated Robert Boyle, who had turned his attention to natural philosophy, and already made great improvements in the air-pump, devised an alteration in what might be called the form of the heat measurer. He left the tube open at both ends, and turned one of them upwards in a curve; this he sealed hermetically, by melting the glass to a vessel, on the top of which a hole was pierced, and the pressure of the atmosphere caused the spirit to rise and descend, in the upright portion of the tube, as the condition of the atmosphere was changed. Boyle, who was a son of the Earl of Cork, was a man distinguished in every way for noble qualities of mind and heart. After travelling through Europe, he settled in England; and during the great civil war which was waged between Charles I. and his Parliament, he had the good fortune to enjoy the favour of several eminent men on both sides; and having thus obtained protection both for person and property, he was enabled to follow his literary and scientific pursuits at leisure and in peace.

Boyle's chemical experiments date from the year 1646; and in all probability it was shortly after this period that he first turned his attention to the improvement of the thermometer. He settled at Oxford in the year 1654, and resided there till 1668, being during that time a member of the association which was then termed "the Invisible College," and which afterwards obtained a permanent existence, and has obtained so much reputation under the title of the Royal Society.

In 1702, Amontons, a French philosopher, invented an air thermometer, which was about four feet long. It consisted of a tube open at both ends, one end turning up, and terminating in a ball with an aperture, so that there was the pressure of two atmospheres on an enclosed column of mercury, which was about twenty-six inches and a half in length. Some spirit, or other similar substance, floated on the top of the mercury; and in this a piece of wire was inserted, while on the top there was an index, which showed the various changes on the scale that was attached to it.

Some of these thermometers were tolerably correct in their working; but they were all defective in one particular, inasmuch as the several expanses of the air are not exactly in proportion to the heat contained in the atmosphere; to remedy this, towards the middle of the seventeenth century the members of an Italian Academy had instruments constructed in which alcohol or spirits of wine was used instead of mercury. In that case the instrument was much like those of the present day. There was a tube with a ball at the bottom of it; and from this ball the air was expelled by heat, and mercury was introduced. The top of the tube was then hermetically sealed; and as the degree of warmth without expanded or contracted the air, the spirit was either raised or depressed in the tube. Alcohol is very sensitive of the influence of heat, and expands very readily under its influence; but it has never been known to be frozen, and these spirit thermometers are therefore well adapted for ascertaining degrees of intense cold; but that very quality prevents it from being a good thermometrical medium for measuring high temperatures, as it boils at 176 degrees of Fahrenheit's scale, or 36 degrees below the point at which ebullition takes place in mercury. It has accordingly been frequently used to ascertain the degree of cold in elevated places; and several of the French philosophers—and the Genevan professor, Saussure, especially—have employed it in the ascent of Mount Blanc and other lofty mountains in the Alpine district of Europe.

Horace Benedict de Saussure, whose father was also a philosopher, was, at the age of twenty-two, appointed to the chair of philosophy in the college of Geneva; and for five-and-twenty years he discharged the duties of a public teacher,—taking advantage of the intervals between his official labours to ascertain the natural phenomena of the sublime and romantic district in which he was born. From his very childhood he had indulged this passion; and before he was eighteen years of age, he had explored the mountains in the neighbourhood of his native place. These excursions only created in him new desires for the indulgence of his curiosity; and he became more eager than ever to explore more closely the lofty heights of the Alpine mountains, on whose barren and exalted summits, and in whose dark and yawning ravines are written the records of the world's history, before man became an inhabitant of the earth, and where nature seems to reign supreme in solemn majesty. At length, in the year 1760, alone, and on foot, he made his way to the glaciers of Chamouni, then little visited even by those who lived in the locality, and which were almost altogether unknown to the world in general.

The ascent and descent were both difficult and dangerous, but it was accomplished in safety; and the next year, Saussure returned to renew his observations. From that time, the spirit of exploration was not to be restrained; and year by year he made not only excursions, but undertook many journeys, to carry on his observations among the mountains, in different parts of Europe.

Between the years 1758 and 1779, he traversed the whole chain of the Alps no less than fourteen different times by

GLACIERS OF CHAMOUNI.

eight different routes, and made sixteen other excursions to the centre of the mountain mass. He went over the Vosps and the Jura, traversed the passes of Switzerland, trod the craggy heights of Germany, surveyed those of England, of Italy, and of Sicily and the adjacent islands, inspected the ancient volcanoes of Auvergne, and visited the mountains of Dauphiné and the other parts of France. And all this he did with his mineralogist's hammer in his hand, clambering up to every peak to observe the various strata, and making his notes on the very spot, where the different peculiarities existed, which he had set out to describe.

In 1787, when forty-seven years of age, he ascended to the top of Mont Blanc, and in the intense cold of that lofty region, surrounded by the winds which howl among the heights and rush down like the blasts that sweep across the stormy ocean, he remained three hours and a half, noting the natural phenomena of that sublime district.

MONTE ROSA.

In the following year, accompanied by his eldest son, he encamped on the Col du Geunt, at a height of 11,170 feet above the level of the sea, and remained there seventeen days without quitting his position, and in the year after he reached the summit of Monte Rosa in the Penine Alps.

During his several journeys, while Saussure naturally turned his attention to the meteorological phenomena, he invented several philosophical instruments, the necessity for which he learned from his personal experience. Among others, a thermometer for ascertaining the temperature of water at great depths, an hygrometer to show the quantity of watery vapour in the atmosphere, and an electrometer to develop its electrical condition.

Up to the time of Sir Isaac Newton, mercury and spirit had been the only materials used for thermometers, but he was dissatisfied with them both, and adopted linseed-oil, a substance which has nearly the same power of expansibility, while it may at the same time be subjected to both very high and low degrees of temperature, without either freezing or boiling. But an almost equal objection existed to the use of oil, for in time it became viscid, and adhered a good deal to the middle of the tube; a fault which prevented the observations being depended upon, and the use of it, consequently, in the construction of thermometers has of late years been entirely discontinued.

Mercury is now the only substance used for thermometers, and its first application has been variously ascribed to Dr. Halley, and Mr. Romer, the discoverer of the motion of light. According to Dr. Boerhaave, Romer invented the mercurial thermometer in 1709, but it was not till 1724 that any knowledge of it was obtained in this country, during which year an account of the thermometer invented by Mr. Fahrenheit, of Amsterdam, was first read to the Royal Society. In that paper it was shown that the mercury more nearly represents the alteration in the amount of heat in the atmosphere, than either alcohol or air. Being easily deprived of the air it contains, and from its metallic quality, and ability to conduct heat rapidly, the change in its volume both quickly and accurately represents the alterations in the atmosphere.

Fahrenheit's thermometer is the one now in general use in this country, although that arranged by M. Reaumur is usually employed in France. The main difference between the two consists in the gradation of the scale—Reaumur fixing his zero at 32 degrees of Fahrenheit, and dividing the ranges between that point and the point of boiling water into 80 degrees, while Fahrenheit takes a scale of 212 degrees between his zero and the boiling point.

It is said that Fahrenheit obtained his zero by having mercury exposed in a tube to intense cold, in Iceland, during the year 1709. He then immersed the tube in freezing water, and found that the mercury stood at the 32nd degree above. On immersing it in boiling water, it stood at 212 degrees.

This scale he obtained by ascertaining the capacity of the bulb, and dividing it into ten thousand parts, he found that the expansion of the mercury was just equal to two hundred and twelve of these parts when it was exposed to boiling water.

The thermometer constructed by Reaumur was a spirit thermometer. He divided the capacity of the ball into one thousand parts, and then marked off the divisions, two of which were equal to one of those parts. He found his zero by exposing the instrument to freezing water; and then plunging it into boiling water, he observed whether the spirit rose to exactly eighty of those divisions, and if it did not he strengthened or diluted the spirit until it rose. But this could give no fair indications of heat, as spirit boils long before it reaches the point of boiling water, and the one now termed Reaumur's thermometer is an improvement upon the instrument constructed by him.

Other kinds of thermometers have been invented for combined purposes. One of the chief of these is rather a barometer and thermometer united in the same instrument. Another, in which coloured sulphuric acid is employed as an indicator, is in fact two thermometers, each having a rectangular addition at the bottom, where the ends are joined and hermetically sealed. There are balls at the upper end of each of the upright tubes, and just as the air contained in each of the balls varies from the other, the spirit rises in the tube in which the air is most rarified.

Such are the several gradations through which one of the most important instruments in the service of the useful arts has been brought to its present state of perfection—one which has rendered invaluable aid in those more abstruse scientific investigations which have resulted in so much benefit to mankind.

THE BAROMETER.

IKE all great discoveries, the Barometer was found out by accident. The Duke of Florence had employed some pump-makers upon his premises, and they found that they could not raise the water above thirty feet, when the air in the tube was exhausted. In their dilemma they applied to the celebrated philosopher Galileo. He replied that nature had no power to destroy a vacuum beyond thirty-two feet; for, learned as Galileo was, he understood not the equipoising weight of atmosphere. It was left to his pupil Torricelli to make this discovery.

Evangelista Torricelli, who in early life distinguished himself for his mathematical and philosophical knowledge, was a native of Piancondoli, in Romagna, where he was born in the year 1608. By the care of an uncle, he received an excellent education at the Jesuit School in Faenza, where he became remarkable for his mathematical and scientific attainments. At twenty years of age his uncle sent him to Rome, and he there became intimate with Castelli, then mathematical professor of the college of that city. About this

EVANGELISTA TORRICELLI.

time Galileo was endeavouring to overturn the received doctrine that substances descended in speed according to their natural gravity; and that consequently, if two weights were to descend from a high position, the one which was ten times the weight of the other would reach the ground ten times as soon. Galileo had discovered the pressure of the atmosphere, and was convinced of the principle of its specific gravity, and of the opposition which it occasioned to the effect of the earth's attraction. He went, attended by several officials, to test its validity, and two stones, of very unequal weight, were dropped from the falling tower in Pisa. The truth was evident from the fact that the stones reached the ground nearly at the same moment; but it was in vain that Galileo pointed out that the difference in the time of their descent was entirely owing to the unequal resistance of the air. Prejudice had darkened reason too much for conviction to enter into the minds of the officials by whom he was accompanied.

These several experiments, and similar facts which had been educed .by them, were too important to be overlooked by the acute mind of Torricelli; and he published two tracts,—one on the motion of fluids, and the other on mechanics,—which soon obtained the favourable notice of the venerable Galileo, by whom he was invited to Florence. After Galileo's death, which shortly took place, the Duke of Florence gave Torricelli the chair of mathematics in the Academy; and he thus became his friend's successor when he was about thirty-nine years of age.

As has been observed, Galileo had ascertained, through the representations of the workmen of the Duke of Florence, that water cannot be raised higher than thirty-two feet in a cylinder when the air is exhausted. With this circumstance Torricelli had also become acquainted; and being desirous of confirming the fact, or of discovering that the assertion was erroneous, he employed a more convenient medium for the purpose than water, and therefore used, in place of it, mercury, which is about fourteen times as heavy. Having closed a glass tube hermetically at one end, he filled it with mercury, and then brought the open end inverted into a vessel partly filled with the same substance, taking care that the end of the tube should be under the surface of the mercury in the open vessel. He thus observed that the column in the tube contracted till the top of it stood at between twenty-nine and thirty inches above the mercury in which it was immersed. Having marked the specific gravity of the mercury, the weight of the column of air between the mercury and the top of the tube became of course apparent, from the respective proportions of the columns of air and mercury and the whole length of the tube. It should be stated, that in 1631, that is, twelve years before Torricelli's observations, Descartes, the French philosopher, had made the same observation, although he does not appear to have turned it to any account.

This was the first and the great step; but whether Torricelli is entitled to the honour of having been the first to discover the true reason of the depression of the mercury, is uncertain; at any rate, there was at once an end of the " vacuum" assertions, and a great step was gained towards sound philosophical principles, and to that merit he is most decidedly entitled.

The subject had excited too much attention to be dropped; and Pascal Mersenne in France, and Boyle in England, took it up. Of these, Pascal appears to have been the most sensible and rational observer. He very reasonably argued, that if it were the column of air which occasioned the alteration of the column of mercury, the higher the point in the atmosphere, the higher the mercury would stand in the tube; and Boyle had well prepared the way for him by testing the barometer with airs of different densities, by means of the air-pump.

To carry this principle to some practical conclusion, Pascal requested his friend, M. Perrier, to ascertain the height at which the mercury stood at the base and on the summit of the Ruy de Dome, one of the loftiest mountains in the province of Auvergne. The result perfectly answered his expectations. At the base, the mercury stood at a height of 26¼ inches, while on the summit it was only 23½ inches; the mountain being between three and four thousand feet above the level of the sea. A like result was afterwards ascertained by Pascal himself; and he also discovered that the same rule prevailed and was very sensibly shown, in the ascent of a private house and a church tower.

Thus the fact was satisfactorily established, that the weight of a column of air was equal to that of a column of mercury about twenty-eight inches high, that is, a pressure of about fifteen pounds on a square inch.

The barometer only required the addition of an index and a weather-glass, to give a fair and true announcement of the state and weight of the atmosphere. The instruments are now manufactured in several different forms, but the principle is the same in all, and repeated observations during the ascent of the loftiest mountains in Europe and America, have confirmed the truth of barometrical announcements; for by its indications, the respective heights of the acclivities in high regions can now be ascertained by means of this instrument better than by any other course, with this advantage, too, that no proportionate height need be known to ascertain the altitude.

In navigation the barometer has become an important element of guidance, and a most interesting incident is recounted by Capt. Basil Hall, indicative of its value in the open sea. While cruising off the coast of South America, in the Medusa frigate, one day, when within the tropics, the commander of a brig in company was dining with him. After dinner, the conversation turned on the natural phenomena of the region, when Captain Hall's attention was accidentally directed to the barometer in the state-room where they were seated, and to his surprise he observed it to evince violent and frequent alteration. His experience told him to expect bad weather, and he mentioned it to his friend. His companion, however, only laughed, for the day was splendid in the extreme, the sun was shining with its utmost brilliance, and not a cloud specked the deep blue sky above. But Captain Hall was too uneasy to be satisfied with bare appearances. He hurried his friend to his ship, and gave immediate directions for shortening the top hamper of the frigate as speedily as possible. His lieutenants and the men looked at him in mute surprise, and one or two of the former ventured to suggest the inutility of the proceeding. The captain, however, persevered. The sails were furled; the top-masts were struck; in short, everything that could oppose the wind was made as snug as possible. His friend, on the contrary, stood in under every sail.

The wisdom of Captain Hall's proceedings was, however, speedily evident; just, indeed, as he was beginning to doubt the accuracy of his instrument. For hardly had the necessary preparations been made, and while his eye was ranging over the vessel to see if his instructions had been obeyed, a dark hazy hue was seen to rise in the horizon, a leaden tint rapidly overspread the sullen waves, and one of the most tremendous hurricanes burst upon the vessels, that ever seaman encountered on his ocean home. The sails of the brig were immediately torn to ribbons, her masts went by the board, and she was left a complete wreck on the tempestuous surf which raged around her, while the frigate was driven wildly along at a furious rate, and had to scud under bare poles across the wide Pacific, full three thousand miles, before it could be said that she was in safety from the blast.

THE TELESCOPE.

WHAT wonders yet remain to be discovered by the Telescope we know not, although every year brings to light some new world by its aid, that had stood unobserved, in the immensity of space, by the eye of man, since the day it was first rolled into the illimitable and starry expanse, at the bidding of the Omnipotent. Through the power of this wonderful instrument the human eye is enabled to sweep through vast systems—a boundless extent of space that, had the swiftest race-horse which ever struck its hoof upon the earth, set out from the orb of Uranus, about three thousand years ago, and plunged on in his headlong course day and night without ceasing, he would not yet have traversed the half of this huge diameter that extends 3,600,000,000 of miles. Even by the sides of our system, where but few stars are visible, the gigantic telescope of the Earl Rosse has been turned, and there firmaments have been discovered like our own, covered with countless stars, seeming in that vast distance like a spot glittering with the dust of thousands of diamonds, one almost appearing to touch another, yet each lying from each millions of miles apart, and every one a huge world to which our own earth bears no more proportion than a single daisy does to the field in which it grows.

By the aid of the telescope we have been enabled to

distinguish objects in the moon ; to see huge volcanoes sending forth their awful fires ; to distinguish mountains ranged pile above pile with vast yawning pits at their feet, some of which appear to be 22,000 feet deep. By it we are enabled to trace the course of the fiery comet, as it goes threading its terrible way between the vast worlds that circle round us, until it is lost in that immense sea of space which, like eternity, seems to have no shore.

The telescope can scarcely be called a discovery ; its construction may, but it was by accident that a poor Dutch spectacle-maker first threw two lenses together in an influential position, and by chance stumbled upon the origin of the most wonderful instrument that was ever perfected by man. " The magnitude of the heavenly bodies," says a writer in the " North British Review," " and their almost infinite distance from us, and from each other, fill the mind with views at once magnificent and sublime, while our ideas of the Creator's power rise with the number and magnitude of his works, and expand with the ever-widening bounds which they occupy. The telescope was a mighty gift which God gave to man, to place before him and beside him new worlds, and systems of worlds, probably the abodes of spirits—the dwellings of saints that have suffered, and of sages that have been truly wise.

" When viewed from the highest peak of a mountainous region, our own globe is the largest magnitude we can perceive, and the circuit of its visible horizon the greatest distance we can scan ; but vast as are these units in relation to the eyeball by which they are seen, they are small when compared with the globe itself, or with its circular outline. The navigator who has measured the earth's circuit by his hourly progress, or the astronomer who has paced a degree of the meridian, can alone form a clear idea of velocity when he knows that light moves through a space equal to the circumference of the earth in the eighth part of a second of time—in the twinkling of an eye.

Bearing in mind this unit of velocity, we are enabled to soar to far higher conceptions. The light of the sun takes 160 minutes to move to the Georgium Sidus, the remotest planet of our solar system; and so vast is the unoccupied space between us and the nearest fixed star, that light would require five years to pass through it, and this, be it remembered, travelling a space vast as the circumference of the earth which we inhabit in the twinkling of an eye. But this space is nothing, compared to the distance of stars which have been discovered by the telescope, which are, beyond doubt, many thousands of times more distant from us than the nearest fixed star, the light of which must have travelled thousands of years before it became visible to us, even by the aid of the telescope. The swiftest messenger that could have been dispatched, had it started from one of these distant stars on the morning of the Mosaic creation, would not yet have reached our own planetary system."

Vast and astounding as this immeasurable distance is, and even when the telescope has discovered the faintest star, whose distance could not be comprehended by the aid of figures, we are still only on the borders of the infinity of space; above, around, and beneath, lie the endless, the dim, and the undiscovered, light, or darkness, or millions of millions of leagues hung with suns, and worlds, and stars, or black, silent, and desolate; into this immensity of space no human eye will ever look, nor no instrument ever be invented to gauge its endless silence.

Before the discovery of the telescope our earth was supposed to be the only planet that had a sun to light it by day, and a moon to shine upon it by night. By it other suns and moons and vast worlds have been discovered, many to which our earth may but be likened as a mole-hill to a mountain. By it the Pleiades, which, to the naked eye, showed only a cluster of seven stars, was discovered by Galileo to contain forty; and in the moon he found, by the aid of this mighty instrument, high mountains, whose summits were gilded by sunshine, and deep valleys, into which the gloomy shadows thrown from these high ranges settled down.

Such is the privilege man obtains by this scientific discovery. It has opened to him the contemplation of the sublime, and yet enabled him to feel that he is still in the region of fact. Men gazed on the starry heavens but to conjecture and to theorize in the most civilized times of old. The instrument was wanting which enables us to guage the depths of space, and to interpret the problems of suns and systems. Printing, which secures the permanence of every discovery, and renders the universal spread of knowledge certain—the steam-engine, which increases the mechanical and locomotive powers of man beyond limit—the mariner's compass, which renders his track across the ocean independent of the celestial lights—seem each of greater value than the telescope, because the advantages they secure to man belong more to his natural dwelling-place. But the wonders unfolded by this instrument, and the true relation of our earth to the vast universe of organized worlds which it opens to him, entitles it to be called his sublimest invention. Yet is it so simple that the reflection still follows us of man's dulness to learn and to seize upon the teachings of nature through a long lapse of ages.

Some knowledge of the properties of a lens, or convex glass, it has been already said, was possessed by the ancient Greeks, but we have no clear intimation of the power of a lens to present objects in greater magnitude than when seen by the naked eye till the thirteenth century. Vitello, an Italian, makes this earliest statement; and soon after our illustrious countryman, Roger Bacon, in his "Opus Majus," plainly speaks of the power of a sphere of glass to augment the apparent size of objects placed before it. There is little doubt but that the combination of two lenses, or of a concave and a convex mirror and a lens, had often been tried between the time of

Roger Bacon (1292) and that of Dr. Dee, who published his preface to "Euclid's Elements" in 1570, which is considered to be the epoch of the real discovery of the powers of the telescope. In that treatise the doctor, who, after speaking of the skill necessary to discover the numerical strength of an enemy's army at a distance, says that a " captain may wonderfully help himself thereto by the use of perspective glasses," by which nothing can be understood but a telescope. That this is the correct conclusion is confirmed by a passage in a work called " Pantometria," written by a person named Digges, which appeared in 1571, and which was brought out by his son twenty years afterwards.

In this work it is shown that by concave and convex mirrors of circular and parabolic forms, or by frames of them placed at certain angles, and using the aid of transparent glasses which may break or unite the images produced by the reflection of the mirrors, there may be represented a whole region ; also, that any part of it may be augmented, so that a small object may be discerned as plainly as if it were close to the observer, though it may be as far distant as the eye can descry.

This is doubtless one of those conceptions of the imagination as to the powers of a new instrument rather than a detail of fact. But be that as it may, it is very evident that before the commencement of the seventeenth century the capability of discerning distant objects with facility through the agency of lenses and mirrors, combined in some way or other, had been decidedly obtained.

That this combination, however, had not been applied to any great purpose of practical utility for many years afterwards, appears to be tolerably evident from the little intimation we have of it during the first half of the seventeenth century. In the year 1655 a work entitled " De Vero Telescopii Inventore" was published at the Hague by Peter Borellius, who was in all probability some relative of Mr. Borell, at that time minister from the Hague to the British Court. In this work he ascribes the invention to two individuals, one named Zachariah Jans, or Jansen, and the other Hans Lippershinn, both of whom were spectacle-makers at Middleburgh. In a letter written by a son of Jansen, it is asserted that the invention was completed in the year 1590, while in other accounts it is stated not to have been made until twenty years afterwards—that is, in 1680. It is also stated that in the year 1610 these two makers, Jansen and Lapprey, presented a telescope to Prince Maurice of Nassau, who desired the invention to be kept secret, as his country was at that time at war with France, and he expected to obtain some advantages over the enemy by ascertaining the number of their forces when at a distance. Descartes, however, gives a different account to this. He says, in his "Dioptrics," that the principle of the telescope had been discovered about thirty years before, that is, about, or soon after, the year 1600, by a person named Metius, a native, or at any rate a resident at Alckmaer, and who was fond of amusing himself with making burning lenses of glass and ice, and who accidentally placed a concave and a convex lens at the end of a tube. At any rate, whoever was the chief inventor of the instrument, the Jansens appear to have been the first to apply it to astronomical purposes; and the younger of the two is said to have been the first to discover the satellites of Jupiter, for he perceived four small stars near that planet, but did not continue his observations long enough to become acquainted with their true character, or at least not sufficiently so to authorize him in publishing his discovery to the world. It is, however, certain that the celebrated mathematician Harriott used a telescope magnifying from one to thirty times, and that with it he discovered, in 1610, the spots upon the sun's disc; but whether he got his instrument from Holland or elsewhere is not specified in his papers.

About the time that the Jansens were surveying the heavens in the Netherlands, Galileo entered upon that field of observation by which his name has been immortalized. He contrived a telescope with a convex object-glass at one end of a leaden tube, and a concave eye-glass at the other. With the first instrument which he made he obtained a magnifying power of three, then he made another of eight, and some time afterwards he obtained a magnifying power of thirty times; and through the aid of these instruments the great philosopher succeeded in making larger contributions to the knowledge of the visible heavens than had ever been made since the days of Ptolemy. Before his time the sun and moon were the only celestial bodies which had been ascertained to possess any particular form or magnitude; for although the stars and the planets were objects with whose appearance men were familiar, the sky only seemed to them to be one great vault of ether, in which they shone in beauty, it is true, but also in uselessness to mankind—vague, uncertain, undefined points in the heavens. But the use of the telescope opens out new views of the economy of the universe. The dim small specks that broke through the misty haze of the atmosphere were discovered to be worlds, or suns in some remote region of space, while the planets were found to be nearer to the earth, and to undergo certain changes, and to be of magnitudes measurable by the human intellect. By the spots upon its surface, the sun was found to revolve on its own axis; and the difference of tint observed in the moon, was found to result from the deep ravines and the lofty mountains on the face of our satellite. In 1610, the same year in which the younger Jansen discovered what were afterwards found to be satellites of Jupiter, although he was not able to define their real nature, Galileo also perceived them, and made out their true character. Shortly afterwards he discovered that there was a remarkable appearance about the planet Saturn, which at first seemed to arise from the neighbourhood of two brilliant stars, but which he afterwards found was occasioned by the existence of a luminous belt or ring by which it was surrounded. Very shortly after this, he perceived that the planet Venus assumed the same kind of phases as the moon.

About the time that Galileo was engaged in his discoveries, public attention was especially directed to astronomy by the appearance of a brilliant star in the constellation Ophiuchus; and Galileo took occasion to propound his notions of the Copernican system. Though certainly not the inventor of the telescope, he was, unquestionably, the first who applied it with any profitable effect to astronomical purposes. The first telescope of Galileo he presented to the Doge of Venice, by whom he was rewarded with a salary of 1,000 florins, and with what was far more estimable in his sight, the professorship of mathematics for life.

One of the favourite but delusive propositions of the middle ages was, that " all that was heavenly was bright and pure," whether material or spiritual. Thus even the learned of Galileo's time believed the heavenly bodies to be all-perfect in their spherical form, self-luminous, and without anything gross about them, or in their nature. Galileo, by the use of his telescope, at once dispelled this delusion, and broke the fetters of the synthetical reasoning of the day. He found that the moon, instead of being a spiritual orb, was no other than an earthy globe like our own; and that she always turned the same face to the earth, so that, except through the influence of what are called her "librations," the whole of one of her hemispheres is hidden from our sight. From the moon, the supposition was carried to the planets, and the rest of the satellites of the solar system. A late achievement of superior intellect combined with mechanical skill—the gigantic telescope of Lord Rosse—has proved to us that the moon is, indeed, a globe of earthy matter, but without either atmosphere or inhabitants, and presenting all the appearance of a vast volcanic *debris*.

Shortly after the period of which we were speaking, Galileo made his next great discovery—that the *Via Lactea*, or Milky Way, was an accumulation of myriads of stars spread through the regions of space. Not long afterwards, he discovered the satellites of Jupiter, and named them "Medicean Stars," in compliment to his patron, Duke Cosmo. By the imperfect though highly useful instruments he possessed, he next perceived the edge of the ring of Saturn, but thought it only two stars, as he failed to observe the rotation of the planet.

These discoveries, instead of procuring for Galileo the honour and respect he deserved, excited the anger and jealousy of many of his contemporaries, by the more bigoted of whom the cry of heresy was raised against him because he published to the world his conviction of the soundness of the Copernican System. On two several occasions his writings were condemned, and a sentence of imprisonment pronounced against him by the Council of the Inquisition, and, in fact, at the time of his death in 1642, and for several years previous, he was confined a prisoner, in his own house, by the order of Pope Urban VIII., who granted this as a mitigation of the more severe sentence passed upon him. It was during one of these imprisonments that Galileo was visited by the poet Milton, then on his travels in Italy, and Milton, in one of his works, speaking of Italy, thus alludes to the circumstance:—"There it was that I found and visited the famous Galileo, grown old, a prisoner to the Inquisition, for thinking in Astronomy otherwise than the Franciscan and Dominican licensers thought."

Since the time of Galileo, telescopes with a single convex glass have been designated as *astronomical* telescopes, because they were chiefly used for surveying the heavenly bodies; but on account of the smallness of the field, or the space in which the object is seen, when these instruments are made of great

MILTON VISITING GALILEO IN PRISON.

magnifying power, they have been almost entirely discontinued for that purpose, and are now used principally for distinguishing objects at a short distance. A manifest improvement upon this instrument was devised by Kepler, who, in his "Dioptrics," suggested that, instead of one, two convex glasses should be used; but he did not carry his design to any practical effect. The credit of having done so seems justly ascribed to Scheiner, a Jesuit, who, writing in 1650, gives a description of a telescope with one convex glass, and states that he had used such an instrument before the Arch-duke Maximilian of Austria, thirteen years prior to that period, but acknowledged that it represented objects in an inverted position. Notwithstanding this defect, instruments with one convex glass were favourites with philosophers, on account of the larger field of view which they afforded; but telescopes with two convex glasses were devised both by Kepler and Scheiner, and presented objects as they are perceived by the naked eye.

In Italy, Joseph Campani formed two refracting telescopes,

e 2

the one thirty-four and the other eighty-six feet long; and it was by these instruments that Dominique Cassini, in 1671-2, discovered the fifth and third satellite of Saturn. Louis XIV. greatly encouraged both the manufactory of Campani and the discoveries of Cassini. Of the former he ordered a telescope 140 feet long, and with it the latter discovered the first and second, or the two smallest, satellites of Saturn; he also first saw the ring of this planet, and discovered and measured the figure of Jupiter with the telescopes made by Cassini.

The next improver of the telescope was Huygens, son of the secretary of three princes of Orange, and brother to the secretary who came with William III. to England in 1688.

Huygens was not only a man of family and education, but of ability and industry. He was the author of several works on mathematics and astronomy, and in the course of his prosecution of the latter science, was the first to ascertain that the two stars, seen by Galileo, in the neighbourhood of the planet Saturn were in reality only the extremities of the circle of the ring (or rather rings, as Sir William Herschel has since discovered them to be) by which that immense globe is surrounded.

Huygens, like all the philosophers of that era, was deeply impressed with the immense value of the telescope for ascertaining the nature, qualities, and functions of the remote objects of creation; and being a good mechanic as well as a philosopher, he turned much of his attention to the improvement of that instrument. His aim was to attain a long focal length to the object-glass, and he succeeded in constructing one of 123 feet, which he afterwards presented to the Royal Society, and with which Dr. Bradley made many of his observations. He fixed an object-glass of the requisite sphere in a frame without a tube, but having joints, so that it could be turned in any direction, at pleasure. This frame was attached to a long pole fixed vertically in the ground, and was directed by the observer to any particular part of the heavens, by means of a string which he held in his hand. Near to the ground there was an eye-glass which could be brought into precisely the same plane with the object-glass; and thus the power for making observations was attained, although there was no tube to connect the two lenses with each other.

By whom the first *reflecting* telescope was invented is not known; but it is probable that as the microscope was improved, that the idea would suggest itself to many minds. The merit has been claimed for our countryman Digges, but without apparently any sufficient foundation, for the first clear notice that we have of such an instrument is contained in a letter from the Père Mersenne to his friend and fellow-student Descartes, and was written about 1639. Mersenne, who was a native of Oyse in the province of Maine in France, and who subsequently became one of the religious order of Minims, was an inmate, for some time, of the college of La Flêche with Descartes; and from the similarity of pursuits, genius, and disposition, there sprung up between them a friendship which they had the great happiness to enjoy without interruption through many years. Mersenne, who afterwards became the superior of his convent, filled the chair of philosophy at Nevers, and was always esteemed a man of great learning and research. Descartes in his reply to his friend discountenanced the idea, and nothing that was practically useful appears to have been effected.

The size and unwieldiness of the instruments at that time in use, proved so great an inconvenience, that philosophers and mechanicians set themselves about obtaining an equal magnifying power in a smaller space. It was suggested that if the image were received in the focus of a paraboidal mirror, and were then observed through a concave lens, that the entire object would be attained. Mr. James Gregory, of Edinburgh, was the first who made the proposition in this country, although he can hardly be said to be its inventor, as the principle had been promulgated by Mersenne in his "Cutoptrics," several years before Gregory wrote. The idea was unquestionably valuable, but it was even then, in 1663, inoperative; for although its author—if he must so be termed, though hardly, as has just been said, entitled to the appellation—came to London for the purpose, he could nowhere meet with an artist who could undertake the formation of such a mirror as he had designed; and the attention of men of science was once more earnestly directed to the improvement of the *dioptric* telescope.

Here again great difficulties had to be encountered; for, after Sir Isaac Newton's discovery of the refragibility of light, it was found that the aberration about the focus of a lens was many hundred times greater than could be accounted for by the form of a glass. As the aberration in a mirror was smaller, and without the chromatic confusion, and consequently much more distinct, Newton set himself to construct such a mirror. Accordingly, early in the year 1669, he obtained a composition of metals likely to suit his purpose, and with his own hands did the greater part of the work for grinding its surface to the form of a sphere. By the year 1677 he had completed two telescopes, an account of which, and the result of the use of them, he sent to the Royal Society, in whose journals it was published. This telescope had a magnifying power of thirty-eight, and the radius of the concave was thirteen inches.

About the same time Mr. Gregory succeeded in accomplishing the design which he had for so many years entertained; and M. Cassegrain, in France, also described the principles on which a reflecting telescope might be made.

Near this period, also, Dr. Hook was engaged in the improvement of the telescope; and in 1674 he produced the first reflecting instrument in which the great speculum was perforated, so that objects might be viewed by looking directly at them, and submitted it to the Royal Society in the February of that year. About 1720, Dr. Bradley, professor of anatomy at Oxford, who had heretofore used, in most of his observations, the long focal instrument of Huygens, applied himself, in conjunction with a gentleman of the name of Molyneux, who resided at Kew, to the improvement of reflecting telescopes, especially with a view to reducing the inconvenient size in which they were made. They succeeded admirably; and having, in 1738, directed two London opticians, Messrs. Hearne and Scarlet, in their mode of construction, these artists were soon enabled to manufacture reflecting telescopes for general use.

Soon after this a maker at Edinburgh, Mr. James Short, was assiduously engaged in the endeavour to form specula, and from his investigations it was ascertained that glass had not sufficient steadiness to preserve a correct parabolic figure; but he succeeded, it is believed, so far as human eye could perceive, in obviating that defect, his telescopes allowing of larger apertures, and of course a better observation of the object.

The improvement of specula, during the whole of the eighteenth century, was sought by all earnest opticians; and, at last, Sir William Herschel, whose numerous discoveries have given him a right to the title of the greatest astronomer after Newton, gave to the reflecting telescope the greatest powers which it had ever up to that time attained. While laboriously engaged in obtaining, as a musician, a daily subsistence, Herschel occupied his leisure hours in the construction of telescopes, both of the Gregorian and of the Newtonian kind; and about 1783, being aided by the liberality of King George III., to whose notice he had been introduced through his discovery of the planet called the *Georgium Sidus*, he set to work to make a telescope of forty feet in focal length, after Newton's principles. He succeeded in fully accomplishing his object in the year 1789; and the very night after its completion he discovered the remote orb which is the sixth satellite of Saturn.

This telescope possesses a magnifying power of 6,500 times, and has, in the hands of Sir William Herschel, and of his son, the present eminent astronomer, Sir John Herschel, proved immensely serviceable in the promotion of astronomical science, and in the improvement of those arts and professions to which it is made subservient.

We must not, however, conclude our description without making honourable mention of another name connected with the improvement of this useful instrument. After Sir William Herschel, came John Ramage, an Aberdeen merchant, who, as early as the year 1806, had made reflectors with specula six inches in diameter. These he improved upon, and, only four years after, produced an instrument with a focal length of eight feet, and a mirror that measured nine inches. Not yet satisfied, he ventured still farther, and from a focal length of twenty feet, with a specula thirteen and a half inches in diameter, he at length completed telescopes twenty-five feet long, with mirrors of fifteen inches. Although these reflecting telescopes showed the double stars very distinctly, yet in no instance did they aid in any new discovery; not even when Ramage had succeeded in making an instrument with a focal length of fifty-four feet, and a speculum twenty-one inches in diameter—a clear proof that the power of the reflecting telescope, as regarded discoveries, could not be carried beyond the improvements made by Herschel.

While the reflecting telescope was thus progressing towards its present state of perfection, the endeavour to diminish the fringe of colours which surrounded the appearance of objects when viewed through dioptric instruments did not cease. An improvement made by Mr. Chester Hall, in 1729, greatly facilitated the attainment of a clear image through the eye-

RAMAGE'S TELESCOPE.

glass. It will be remembered that he endeavoured to accomplish that object by using lenses of different kinds of glass; and his idea was further carried out by the celebrated optical instrument-maker and philosopher Mr. Dolland, about thirty years afterwards. In consequence of strictures made upon some observations which he published in the "Philosophical Transactions," on a proposition of Euler's to use hollow spherical segments of glass with water between them, to diminish the aberration in telescopes, Mr. Dolland was led to make experiments on wedges of different kinds of glass to ascertain the various degrees of refragibility which they occasioned. He ultimately discovered that by using a convex lens of crown glass, and a concave lens of flint glass, the different coloured rays in each pencil of light, after refraction through both, fell upon the eye nearly colourless. For this improvement he was presented with the Copleian medal by the Royal Society; and a few years afterwards, in 1765, his son, Mr. Peter Dolland, made a still further improvement by diminishing the aberration occasioned by the spherical form of the glass. He placed a concave lens of flint glass between two convex lenses of crown glass, an arrangement which almost altogether did away with the fringed coloration of the image, and gave the still further advantage of a large aperture for the observation of the object when the focal strength of the instrument is short.

Various improvements were afterwards made by Mr. Ramsden and others, chiefly with a view to destroy the aberration through the union of spheres of different kinds of glass. But the greatest triumph that ever was achieved in the conjunction of philosophical acumen and mechanical skill, has been accomplished in our own day, and through the agency of a nobleman whose name will live as long as the human faculties shall be exercised in observing the magnificent wonders of the central universe. This is the monster telescope constructed by Lord Rosse.

To give a description of this wonderful instrument would, within our limits, be an utter futility, for it deserves a separate and entire volume; but the following account, first sent to the "Times," by Sir James South, will convey some idea of its power and magnitude.

"The diameter of the large speculum is 6 feet, its thickness $5\frac{1}{4}$ inches, its weight $3\frac{3}{4}$ tons, and its composition 126 parts of copper to $57\frac{1}{4}$ parts of tin; its focal length is 54 feet—the tube is of deal; its lower part, that in which the speculum is placed, is a cube of 8 feet; the circular part of the tube is, at its centre,

LORD ROSSE'S MONSTER TELESCOPE.

7¼ feet diameter, and at its extremities, 6¼ feet. The telescope lies between two stone walls, about 71 feet from north to south, about 50 feet high, and about 23 feet asunder. These walls are as nearly as possible parallel with the meridian.

"In the interior face of the eastern wall, a very strong iron arc, of about 43 feet radius, is firmly fixed, provided, however, with adjustments, whereby its surface facing the telescope may be set very accurately in the plane of the meridian—a matter of the greatest importance, seeing that by the contact with it of rollers attached to one extremity of a quadrangular bar, which slides through a metal box fixed to the under part of the telescope tube, a few feet from the object end of the latter, whilst its other extremity remains free, the position of the telescope in the meridian is secured, or any deviation from it easily determined, for on this bar lines are drawn, the interval between any adjoining two of which corresponds to one minute of time at the equator. The tube and speculum, including the bed on which the latter rests, weigh about 15 tons.

107

"The telescope rests on a universal joint, placed on masonry, about 6 feet below the ground, and is elevated or depressed by a chain and windlass; and, although it weighs about 15 tons, the instrument is raised by two men with great facility. Of course, it is counterpoised in every direction.

"The observer, when at work, stands in one of four galleries, the three highest of which are drawn out from the western wall, whilst the fourth, or lowest, has for its base an elevating platform, along the horizontal surface of which a gallery slides from wall to wall, by machinery within the observer's reach, but which a child may work.

"When the telescope is about half an hour east of the meridian, the galleries hanging over the gap between the walls, present to a spectator below an appearance somewhat dangerous; yet the observer, with common prudence, is as safe as on the ground, and each of the galleries can be drawn from the wall to the telescope's side so readily, that the observer needs no one else to move it for him.

"The telescope lying at its least altitude can be raised to the zenith by the two men at the windlass in six minutes; and so manageable is the enormous mass, that, give me the right ascension and declination of any celestial object between these points, and I will have the object in the field of the telescope within eight minutes from the first attempt to raise it.

"When the observer has found the object, he must at present follow it by rack-work within his reach. As yet, it has no equatorial motion, but it very shortly will, and at no very distant day clock-work will be connected with it, when the observer, if I mistake not, will, whilst observing, be almost as comfortable as if he were reading at a desk by his fireside."

It commands an immense field of vision, and it is said that objects as small as one hundred yards cube can be observed at a distance of 240,000 miles by it in the moon, so that it may be expected that our satellite will speedily become well known to us.

By the aid of this mighty instrument, what astronomers have before called nebula, on account of their cloud-like appearance, have been discovered to be stars or suns, with planets moving round them, like those which revolve round our own sun. In the constellations Andromeda and the sword-hilt of Orion, both of which are visible to the naked eye, these cloud-like patches have been seen as clusters of stars. Professor Nichol, in speaking of these discoveries, says, "What mean those dim spots which, unknown before, loom in greater and greater numbers on the horizon of every new instrument, unless they are gleams it is obtaining, on its own frontier, of a mighty infinitude beyond, also studded with glories, and unfolding what is seen as a minute and subservient part? Yes—even the six-feet mirror, after its powers of distinct vision are exhausted, becomes, in its turn, simply as the child gazing on these mysterious lights with awful and hopeless wonder. I shrink below the conception which here—even at this threshold of the attainable—bursts forth on my mind. Look at a cloudy speck in Orion, visible, without aid, to the well-trained eye; that is a stellar universe of majesty altogether transcendent, lying at the verge of what is known. And if any of these lights from afar, on which the six-feet mirror is now casting its longing eye, resemble in character that spot. the systems from which they come are situated so deep in space that no ray from them could reach our earth until after travelling through the intervening abysses, during centuries whose number stuns the imagination. There must be some regarding which that faint illumination informs us, not of their present existence, but only that assuredly they were, and sent forth into the infinite the rays at present reaching us, at an epoch further back into the past than this momentary lifetime of man, by at least thirty millions of years!"

"When we consider the successive steps of Lord Rosse's progress," says a writer in the Review we have before named,

" we can scarcely doubt that with his hands so skilful, and his head so stored with the chemistry of fusion, and the physics of annealing, lenses of flint and crown glass may yet be executed of gigantic magnitude. In cherishing these high expectations we have not forgotten that the state of our atmosphere must put some limit to the magnifying power of our telescopes. In our variable climate, indeed, the vapours, and local changes of temperature, and consequent inequalities of refraction, offer various obstructions to the extension of astronomical discovery. But we must meet the difficulty in the only way in which it can be met. The astronomer cannot command a thunder-storm to cleanse the atmosphere, and he must, therefore, undertake a pilgrimage to better climates, to Egypt or to India, in search of a purer medium; or even to the flanks of the Himalaya and the Andes, that he may erect his watch-tower above the grosser regions of the atmosphere. In some of these brief but lucid intervals which precede or follow rain, when the remotest objects present themselves in sharp outline and minute detail, discoveries of the highest value might be grasped by the astronomer. The revolution of a nebula, the direction of a double star, the details of a planet's ring, the evanescent marking on its disc, or perhaps the display of some of the dark worlds of Bessel, might be the revelations of a moment, and would amply repay the transportation of a huge telescope to the shoulder or to the summit of a lofty mountain.

" In looking back upon what the telescope has accomplished; in reckoning the thousands of celestial bodies which have been detected and surveyed; in reflecting on the vast depths of ether which have been sounded, and on the extensive fields of sideral matter out of which worlds and systems of worlds are forming, and to be formed—can we doubt it to be the Divine plan that man shall yet discover the whole scheme of the visible universe, and that it is his individual duty, as well as the high prerogative of his order, to expound its mysteries and develop its laws. Over the invisible world he has received no commission to reign, and into its secrets he has no authority to look. It is over the material and the visible that he has to sway the intellectual sceptre; it is among the structures of organic and inorganic life that his functions of combination and analysis are to be chiefly exercised. Nor is this task unworthy of his genius, or unconnected with his destiny. Placed upon a globe already formed, and constituting part of a system already complete, he can scarcely trace, either in the solid masses around him, or in the forms and movements of the planets, any of those secondary causes by which these bodies have been shaped and launched on their journey. But in the distant heavens, where creation seems to be ever active, where vast distance gives us the vision of huge magnitudes, and where extended operations are actually going on, we may study the cosmogony of our system, and mark, even during the brief span of human life, the formation of a planet in the consolidation of the nebulous mass which surrounds it."

OW wondrous is the power of the eye! The immense expanse of sky and ocean— the crowds and buildings of a city—the woods and hills and streams of a landscape—are all séen by it with the same distinctness with which it marks the forms and hues and dimensions of the minute flower or insect. It is the most valuable of our organs of sense, and our admiration of the wondrous adaptations of the universe we inhabit is increased by the fact that light is provided for this organ. Through the aid of light, the figure of any object is pictured on the retina of the eye, just in proportion to its distance. It is upon what philosophers call the "incidence of light" that our vision thus depends.

From the extremities of every object rays are carried to the centre of the human pupil, or sight portion of the eye-ball. Now, lines drawn from the extremities of an object to the eye must describe a triangle, of which the object forms one side The more distant the object, the longer must the sides of the triangle be, and the smaller the object will appear; the nearer it is, the shorter will be the sides, the greater will be the angle, and the larger will be the apparent size of the objects observed.

It is on this principle that both miscroscopes and telescopes are formed. By the intervention of a lens, or of a convex glass, it was perceived that the rays of light passed through it were made to converge, through the concentrating power of the glass, very rapidly to a given point. If these rays converge to the inside, they, of course, diverge towards the outside. If a lens or a spherical piece of glass, therefore, be placed between the eye and any object within a short distance, the natural result will be that large angular rays will be formed between it and the eyes of the observer, and thus all its parts will be greatly magnified in appearance. These rays are called *pencils*, not only because they draw the object on the eye, but also from their figure.

This is the peculiarity of the microscope; and the next object to be attained in its construction, after the magnifying power, is the clearness with which it can be perceived. The principle is much the same in the telescope; and the chief difference to be observed in the two instruments appears to be that in the microscope the main object is to obtain intensity at a short distance, and in the telescope the cumulation of power through a long focal length: that is, to make the distance between the eye of the observer and the place where the rays would diverge to either side of the object, as long as possible. For the longer the focal length, the greater will be the cumulative and penetrative power of the glass; and the introduction of several glasses, as is the case in the best instruments, is only made for the purpose of strengthening the effect.

The inventor of the microscope is utterly unknown. That the ancients made some powerful applications of the lens is evident from the account given by Lucian and Galen that Archimedes burned the Roman fleet, at the siege of Syracuse, by means of glasses, two hundred and twelve years before our era. Yet neither the Greeks nor Romans have left us any account of the lens being applied to increase the stores of discovery in natural science; and the only authentic records we have respecting the microscope belong to its later improvements.

The most useful lenses employed have always been made of glass; though for some time it was believed that precious stones, from their greater refractive power, would make the better lenses. But it was discovered that the substance of precious stones caused such an aberration of the rays of light, that no sufficiently definite object could be observed, and they were consequently disused. It may be briefly observed, that the chief object of a microscope is attained by the disposition of a number of the glass lenses, and the difficulty lies in concentrating the rays of light upon the object-glass.

This was accomplished in a very considerable degree by Dr. Wollaston, who invented what is called his *doublet*. This consisted of two lenses, having one side flat and the other convex, with two pieces of flat glass placed between them. The two lenses were placed so as to present their flat sides towards the object. To this there were several objections; but it was still very superior to the single lens, and will transmit a pencil of light from 35 to 50 degrees, without any very perceptible errors. Dr. Wollaston was led to this discovery by the "eye-piece" constructed for the purpose of obtaining a distinct view of the heavenly bodies by the celebrated philosopher Huygens, by whom it was applied to the telescope only, which had the effect of preventing the appearance of those rays which so often tend to confuse the aspect of any luminous bodies, and which exhibits many objects very beautifully.

The next improvement was made by a gentleman of the name of Holland, who to the lens nearest the object added a smaller one, which had the effect of still further correcting the aberration and concentrating the sight on the real object to be observed. But one misfortune attended this increase of the number of lenses: they necessarily absorbed a portion of the light, and it was soon perceived that three lenses were as many as could be used in the construction of a simple microscope.

Some advantage was obtained by the use of Dr. Wollaston's periscopic lens. This consisted of two hemispheric lenses connected together by their flat faces, an aperture being made between them, which was filled with opaque matter; and Mr. Coddington effected the same object in a better manner, by hollowing out a space of a complete sphere, and then filling it up as Dr. Wollaston had previously done.

But in the construction of a microscope the light under which the object is seen is almost of as much importance as the magnifying power itself; and in the investigation of every unknown substance, it ought to be placed in every possible position to receive the strongest luminence. It should be observed both wet and dry, immersed in such fluids as are best adapted to show its texture, such as water, alcohol, oil, and Canada balsam, which last has itself a power of refraction almost equal to that of glass. In some cases even it will be necessary to place the object between two glasses, and gently heat it to bring out the finer colours and fibres, and in this way the spiral vessels of asparagus and other similar vegetables may be very beautifully displayed.

The simple microscope is occasionally formed with three lenses, but a great improvement was effected when what is called the *compound microscope* was invented. In the latter instrument there are only two lenses, but they are so disposed as to give a cumulative magnitude to the object submitted for inspection. The first lens gathers the rays of light, and presents the object in its apparently increased size, and the second lens then magnifies the reflected object as if it were the original one, preserving all its power, and losing seemingly little by aberration; but yet the aberration and the confusion about the object was sufficient to be an important disadvantage, and for more than a century the compound microscope

115

remained without any improvement. But within the last fifteen years such improvements have been made in the compound microscope as have elevated it to the position of one of the most important instruments that has ever been applied to the promotion of human welfare.

About the year 1820 M. Sallignes in France began a series of experiments for the construction of what is called an achromatic object-glass. M. Chevalier in Paris, Signor Amici at Modona, Herr Frauenhofer at Munich, and Mr. Tulley in London, were at the same time engaged in a similar series of practical operations, and the latter gentleman, without knowing what had been effected on the Continent, succeeded in the construction of an instrument in which the achromatic object-glass, of nine-tenths of an inch focal length, had eighteen degrees of pencil.

Mr. Tulley was the first person in England who attained this object, and he succeeded in making a lens that would bear an eye-piece fitted to produce a magnifying power of one hundred and twenty. He afterwards invented a combination to be placed before that last mentioned, and which increased the angle of the pencil to thirty-eight degrees. He thus obtained a magnifying power of three hundred; and his glass, so far as accurate correctness of the field goes, has not been excelled by any subsequent invention.

While these several improvements were being made by the men practically engaged in the manufacture of philosophical apparatus, the attention of the most eminent persons engaged in the study of the pure sciences was assiduously turned to the same object. Professor Barlow, Mr. Coddington, Professor Airy, and Sir John Herschel, did much towards unfolding the true mathematical principles of the action of light and of the visual organs.

But the individual who was most successful in developing the abstruse doctrines on which the compound microscope was to be most advantageously improved, was Mr. Jackson Lister, a gentleman who had long turned his attention to scientific subjects, although he was neither professionally nor com-mercially engaged in the manufacture of instruments. In a paper which he transmitted to the Royal Society in 1829, and which was published in their transactions of that year, he laid down the real facts which occur in the transmission of rays of light through lenses made of various substances. The details into which he entered are too various, too numerous, and too abstruse to be interesting in such a publication as this; and such as could only be made intelligible by a number of diagrams and a full treatise on the properties of light as reflected from various substances, and refracted in various media. It may therefore be sufficient to observe that such an advance had been made by Mr. Lister's discoveries and explanations, that Mr. Andrew Ross and Mr. Hugh Powell succeeded in making instruments of so perfect a combination, that the object-glass gave a complete achromatic view to the observer. To such a degree of delicacy indeed did they attain, that the interposition of a piece of common glass or of the thinnest talc was sufficient to affect the correctness of the view.

One defect attended this arrangement. The instrument, if it may be so said, was too perfect; for the slightest accidental interruption materially interfered with the delicacy of the results which it presented. Mr. Ross therefore set himself to work to discover the *rationale* of the interfering causes, and in the 51st volume of the Transactions of the Society of Arts published the whole of the principles of, and detailed the means for, obtaining such counter aberrations; and at length succeeded in establishing the basis on which future corrections or improvements can be made.

The object-glass and the lenses, and their adaptation and position, having been brought to this state of perfection, the next object was to improve the eye-glass; and for that purpose

Mr. Varley applied the eye-piece of Huygens, the philosopher who in the seventeenth century had first adopted it to decrease the chromatic aberration of the telescope. The object of Huygens, who was one of the first persons who brought the telescope to such a position as led to its ultimate great improvement, was simply to increase the refractive power of the instrument. For this purpose he placed two plano-convex lenses—that is, a lens flat on one side and convex on the other— at a certain distance from each other, so as to accumulate their magnifying power; and the doing away with the rays, dimness, and uncertain colour of the objects viewed through these lenses, was altogether an accidental discovery. It is indeed even now allowed to be the best for all telescopic purposes; but a further improvement was added by Ramsden and called, from the end which it answered, the *micrometer* eye-piece. When it is recollected that it is frequently necessary to measure objects with dimensions at least a hundred times less than the markings on our finest rules for measurement, the advantage of applying a scale to the magnified object will be sufficiently apparent.

The grander revelations of the microscope all belong to the present century. Swammerdam and Leuwenhoeck, even with imperfect instruments, carried on the most patient and success-ful investigations into animal and vegetable nature; but our discoveries by the microscope, as now improved, transcend all the wondrous accounts they published. By this instrument we learn that every department of nature teems with animal-culæ or with minute vegetable life; and that all are of the utmost importance in the economy of our earth, though not beheld by the naked eye. It has proved to us that classes of animals exist in which the second generation differs from the first in form and habit, the third one taking on the figure of the first, whilst the fourth again is similar to the second, and incredible as it may appear, such is the fact. The human eye, heart, brain, muscles, skin, and other parts of the body are

118

now discovered to be regions of animalcule life. All the larger animals carry numbers upon numbers within or without their bodies. A handful of dried herbs steeped in water will be found, in a few hours, to have produced millions of these living creatures, so small that five hundred millions of them may be contained in one drop of water. Flint, gravel, and chalk beds are found to be formed of their dead bodies; and the composition of the globe seems likely eventually to be traced to their tribes.

"The comparative anatomist," observes the writer of a popular treatise on the microscope, " makes use of this instrument to determine from the structure of the teeth, the form, habit, and class, of animals which lived and have become extinct on our earth for many thousand years. Thus Professor Owen, from the examination of the structure of the tooth of the megatherium, by demonstrating the identity of the dental structure with that of the sloth, has yielded us an unerring indication of the true nature of its food. By the aid of high-power magnifying glasses, we are informed that our island was once possessed of a climate nearly approaching to a tropical one; for if we examine a piece of drift-wood, found in the *eocene* clay (so called from its being the dawn of a new creation) of the estuary of the Thames, we shall find that these fragments belong to a class of plants nearly allied to the pepper tribe, and that they flourished in company with the turtles, vultures, crocodiles, and boa-constrictors of the Sheppey district.

"Every department of nature teems with minute objects of animal and vegetable life, which are of the utmost importance in the economy of this earth, and which are totally unrecognisable by the naked vision. Many of these animals and vegetables are unrivalled for the beauty and complexity of their forms. Some are productive of great changes, which have been effected, or are still going on, in the earth's surface; and some are productive of the greatest mischief and destruction. To illustrate the former, we need only mention the filling up now going on in the harbours of Wismar and Pillau, in the Baltic; and the production of coral-reefs, and their gradual conversion into new islands. The potato disease is an instance of devastation now going on, and is said to be caused by the development of a minute microscopic fungus in the cells of the tubers of this vegetable."

The celebrated Dr. Chalmers thus speaks of the wonders discovered by the microscope:—"While the *telescope* enables us to see a system in every star, the *microscope* unfolds to us a world in every atom. The one instructs us that this mighty globe, with the whole burthen of its people and its countries, is but a grain of sand in the vast field of immensity—the other, that every atom may harbour the tribes and families of a busy population. The one shows us the insignificance of the world we inhabit—the other redeems it from all its insignificance, for it tells us, that in the leaves of every forest, in the flowers of every garden, in the waters of every rivulet, there are worlds teeming with life, and numberless as are the stars of the firmament. The one suggests to us, that above and beyond all that is visible to man, there may be regions of creation which sweep immeasurably along, and carry the impress of the Almighty's hand to the remotest scenes of the universe—the other, that within and beneath all that minuteness which the aided eye of man is able to explore, there may be a world of invisible beings; and that, could we draw aside the mysterious veil which shrouds it from our senses, we might behold a theatre of as many wonders as astronomy can unfold—a universe within the compass of a point, so small, as to elude all the powers of the microscope, but where the Almighty Ruler of all things finds room for the exercise of His attributes, where he can raise another mechanism of worlds, and fill and animate them all with evidences of His glory."

THE MARQUIS OF WORCESTER'S FIRST IDEA OF THE STEAM-ENGINE.

THE MARQUIS OF WORCESTER AND MARIAN DELORME MEETING WITH DE CAUS IN THE BICÊTRE.

THE STEAM-ENGINE.

THE power of steam far surpasses all the fabulous wonders which imaginative genius has attributed to the genii of the East, or the invisible fairies who are made to perform such marvels in our old English legends. The very elements are conquered by this mighty agency; both wind and tide may oppose, but still the vessel plunges onward in spite of all opposition, paddling away against breeze and billow, like some extinct monster of the early world, armed with those sweeping fins that fill the mind of the geologist with wonder and awe. Time and space—those barriers which no mortal power has hitherto overleaped—are now borne down before it, and, in the beautiful language of Scripture, we seem "to ride upon the wings of the wind;" and however rapid may be the march of time, we can almost tell to an instant when we shall overtake him, and tread in his footsteps. This new-born giant thrusteth his iron arm into the bowels of the earth, and throws up its treasures by thousands of tons, emptying the dark mine of its wealth, then leaping on the surface, melting with its hot breath the weighty metal, and rolling and beating it out into massy bars, or drawing it through its crushing fingers until it becomes almost as thin as a lady's girdle. As if struck by the wand of a magician, the iron vessel springs out of the shapeless mass of ore, by the power of steam is launched upon the deep, and stands, as if in mockery, beside its oak-built rival, every rib of which was the growth of a long century. The very leaves that rustle in our hand while we read were formed by it, and every letter in the large sheet of news bears the imprint of its majestic footstep. Even printing, the grandest of all human inventions, was but in comparison the slow copying of the clerk, beside this ready-writer, which now throws off its thousands of perfect impressions within the brief space of a single hour. It grinds the bread we eat, and gives all the variety and beauty to the garments we wear. It stamps the wreath of flowers upon the flimsy foundation of cotton, and sets ten thousand wheels in motion, every stroke of which would grind the human form to powder. And yet the whole of this moving destruction can be stopped in a moment by the hand of a child, when once shown where to place its tiny fingers. The invention of Printing gave power to the human mind to achieve new triumphs over ignorance and vice, and by means of the steam-engine every element of Nature, wherein opposition seemed ever ready to spring forth and defy or overwhelm man, is now bound and overpowered.

Yet, while contemplating the grandeur of the discovery, we are humbled, as in the instance of other great inventions, by the remembrance that so many centuries of human history have passed away during which the powers of steam—an

element almost perpetually within the observation of men—
were, although perceived, unemployed. " What might the
world have become, by this time, had the wonderful capabilities
of steam been known to the nations of antiquity !" is a natural
exclamation ;' but reflection on the nature of man, and his slow
advancement in the great path of fact and science, will, at
once, hush the expression of our wondering regret over the
Past,—while a nobler and more cheering occupation for the
mind, offers itself in speculation on the glorious Future. Let
us attend to the history of this all important invention, as a
means of assisting our calculations of the mighty issues of
that civilization which is now begun.

But in order to understand aright the beautiful simplicity
of the means by which such great changes have been wrought
in the world, it is necessary to explain what steam is, and the
manner in which it acts in propelling the ingenious machines
to which it is applied.

Every one has seen a common tea-kettle upon the fire,
with a white stream of vapour pouring from the spout, and
most people have also observed that the more furiously the
water boils, the more energetically the stream of vapour
pours forth. This is the natural result of the application
of heat to water, for as the bottom of the vessel, which is
nearest the water, first feels the effects of the heat, those
effects are next communicated to the water immediately near
to it. As this grows warm the heat is communicated to the
next globules, and so the process goes on until it is diffused
through the whole quantity of water. As that grows hotter
and hotter at the bottom of the vessel, particles expand until
they assume the form of vapour ; and these being lighter than
the water, gradually force their way through the globules at the
sides, until they reach the surface, where they are partially
condensed into water again, and partly remain in the condition
of vapour, unable to overcome the resistance of the atmosphere,

A 2   3

which presses, with a weight of fifteen pound on the square inch, above them. As the number of these vaporous globules increases, the sound of their propulsion against the globules of air accumulates until it becomes audible at a little distance, and then we hear what is called *singing*.

As the heat still continues to be applied to the water, this expansion of it gradually increases until it is diffused through the whole body in the vessel, and the disturbance is shown in the upheaving and tumultuous agitation of the surface, and the water appears in a state of ebullition, or is what we call *boiling*. As the boiling goes on, the number of globules of water which are expanded into steam increase so much that the force overcomes the weight of the superincumbent atmosphere, and the steam pours forth.

In Dr. Lardner's valuable work on the steam-engine he furnishes us with the following interesting examples of the motive power of a pint of water, when converted by the consumption of two ounces of coal into steam :—" A pint of water," he informs us, " may be evaporated by two ounces of coals. In its evaporation it swells into two hundred and sixteen gallons of steam, with a mechanical force sufficient to raise a weight of thirty-seven tons a foot high. The steam thus produced has a pressure equal to that of common atmospheric air ; and by allowing it to expand, by virtue of its elasticity, a further mechanical force may be obtained, at least equal in amount to the former. A pint of water, therefore, and two ounces of common coal, are thus rendered capable of doing as much work as is equivalent to seventy-four tons raised a foot high."

In relation to the consumption of fuel Dr. Lardner observes :—" The circumstances under which the steam-engine is worked on a railway are not favourable to the economy of fuel. Nevertheless, a pound of coke burned in a locomotive engine will evaporate about five pints of water. In their

4

evaporation they will exert a mechanical force sufficient to draw two tons weight on the railway a distance of one mile in two minutes. Four horses working in a stage-coach on a common road are necessary to draw the same weight the same distance in six minutes.

"A train of coaches weighing about eighty tons, and transporting two hundred and forty passengers with their luggage, has been taken from Liverpool to Birmingham, and back from Birmingham to Liverpool, the trip each way taking about four hours and a quarter, stoppages included. The distance between these places by the railway is ninety-five miles. This double journey of one hundred and ninety miles is effected by the mechanical force produced in the combustion of four tons of coke, the value of which is about five pounds. To carry the same number of passengers daily between the same places by stage-coaches on a common road, would require twenty coaches and an establishment of three thousand eight hundred horses, with which the journey in each direction would be performed in about twelve hours, stoppages included.

"The circumference of the earth measures twenty-five thousand miles; and if it were begirt with an iron railway, such a train as above described, carrying two hundred and forty passenger, would be drawn round it by the combustion of about thirty tons of coke, and the circuit would be accomplished in five weeks.

"In the drainage of the Cornish mines the economy of fuel is much attended to, and coals are there made to do more work than elsewhere. A bushel of coals usually raises forty thousand tons of water a foot high; but it has on some occasions raised sixty thousand tons the same height. Let us take its labour at fifty thousand tons raised one foot high. A horse worked in a fast stage-coach pulls against an average resistance of about a quarter of a hundredweight. Against this he is able to work at the usual speed through about eight miles daily; his work is therefore equivalent to one thousand tons raised one foot. A bushel of coals consequently, as used in Cornwall, performs as much labour as a day's work of one hundred such horses.

" The great pyramid of Egypt stands upon a base measuring seven hundred feet each way, and is five hundred feet high, its weight being twelve thousand seven hundred and sixty millions of pounds. Herodotus states, that in constructing it one hundred thousand men were constantly employed for twenty years. The materials of this pyramid would be raised from the ground to their present position by the combustion of about four hundred and eighty tons of coals.

" The Menai bridge consists of about two thousand tons of iron, and its height above the level of the water is one hundred and twenty feet. Its mass might be lifted from the level of the water to its present position by the combustion of four bushels of coals."

It may cause the reader some surprise to be informed that the discovery of the fact that a mechanical force is produced when water is evaporated by the application of heat (the first capital step in the invention of the steam-engine), is very nearly two thousand years old, having been first pointed out by Hero of Alexandria one hundred and twenty years before the Christian Era. Our young reader will doubtless regard it as almost an equal matter for surprise that this important discovery should have slumbered, as it were, for nearly seventeen hundred years before any application of it to practical uses was attempted, and for upwards of another hundred years before such application even to the most limited extent proved successful. It was about a century and a half ago that a steam-engine, constructed on an imperfect principle, was first used for the raising of water out of mines, which, though much improved upon during the next eighty years, was not sought to be applied to any other purpose. It is from the time of the grand discoveries of Watt that the application of steam power to the extensive and varied uses to which it is now adapted must date its commencement, and the rapidity with which the most important results have been brought about by its agency during the last few years, would seem to compensate in a measure for the many centuries of time which had elapsed before the importance of the discovery of the Grecian philosopher had been made apparent, and the advantages resulting from it applied to the requirements of our own progressive age.

The machine invented by Hero of Alexandria, which was moved by the mechanical force of the vapour of water, is supposed to have been constructed on the following principle. A hollow globe or ball was placed on pivots at A and B, on which

7

it was capable of revolving; steam was supplied from a boiler through the horizontal tube at the bottom of the machine, which tube communicated with the pivot B. This steam filled the globe and also the numerous arms attached to it; while a lateral orifice at the end of each of these arms allowed the steam to escape in a jet. The reaction consequent on this produced a recoil and drove the arms round; if therefore there had been a pulley, as represented, at the upper part of the machine c, with a strap passing round it, the effect would have been to set any machinery in motion to which the other end of the strap might have been attached. This machine, after a lapse of nearly two thousand years, appears to have been recently revived, and rotatory engines, constructed on the same principle and resembling Hero's in many of their details, are now working in this country.

"Among other amusing anecdotes showing the knowledge which the ancients had of the mechanical force of steam, it is related that Anthemius, the architect of Saint Sophia, occupied a house next door to that of Zeno, between whom and Anthemius there existed a feud. To annoy his neighbour, Anthemius placed on the ground floor of his own house several close digesters, or boilers, containing water. A flexible tube proceeded from the top of each of these, which was conducted through a hole made in the wall between the houses, and which communicated with the space under the floors of the rooms in the house of Zeno. When Anthemius desired to annoy his neighbour, he lighted fires under his boilers, and the steam produced by them rushed in such quantity and with such force under Zeno's floors, that they were made to heave with all the usual symptoms of an earthquake."

It is also recorded "that upon the banks of the Weser the ancient Teutonic gods sometimes marked their displeasure by a sort of thunder-bolt, which was immediately succeeded by a cloud that filled the temple. An image of the god *Busterich*,

8

which was found in some excavations, clearly explains the manner in which this prodigy was accomplished by the priests. The head of the metal god was hollow, and contained within it a pot of water: the mouth, and another hole, above the forehead, were stopped by wooden plugs; a small stove, adroitly placed in a cavity of the head, under the pot, contained charcoal, which being lighted, gradually heated the liquid contained in the head. The vapour produced from the water having acquired sufficient pressure, forced out the wooden plugs with a loud report, and they were immediately followed by two jets of steam, which formed a dense cloud round the god, and concealed him from his astonished worshippers."

In 1826, Thomas Gonzales, director of the Archives at Simanghas, in Spain, published copies of documents which he had found in the repository of the national records, and which purported to describe the result of an experiment tried in the harbour of Barcelona in the year 1543, during the reign of the Emperor Charles V.

Some time before, a naval captain, named Blasco de Garay, had made propositions to that monarch of a means by which he could carry ships out of or into harbour against wind or tide; and Charles ordered experiments to be made in the port of Barcelona, in the presence of public commissioners. Accordingly, on the 17th of June in that year, De Garay appeared on the quay with his apparatus moored alongside. He took the utmost pains to conceal the nature of the invention, but it was perceived that the chief apparatus was a cauldron of boiling water and two wheels, one on each side of the vessel to be moved. The experiment answered in every respect. The vessel was found to progress at the rate of a league an hour, or, according to Rarago, the treasurer, who was one of the commissioners (but unfriendly to the design), at the rate of three leagues in two hours; but it *did* progress, and was found to be easily under command and turned with facility to any point

9

where it was directed. Favourable reports were made to the emperor and to his son Philip II., but an expedition in which they were at that time engaged prevented the carrying out of the design to any practical extent. Thus the world was in all probability deprived for two centuries from reaping the immense advantages that would have resulted from the adoption of steam navigation.

At the conclusion of the experiment, De Garay, who was determined to keep his invention perfectly secret, immediately removed his machinery, leaving nothing but the bare wooden framework behind. This discovery, however, was thought so highly of that he was rewarded with promotion and two hundred thousand maravedis, besides having his expenses allowed him.

In the year 1615 a work appears to have been published at

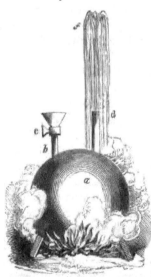

Frankfort, written by Solomon De Caus, an eminent French mathematician and engineer, from a passage in which M. Arago, a distinguished living philosopher, claims for its author a share of the honour of the invention of the steam-engine. De Caus was at one time in the service of Louis the Thirteenth, and afterwards in that of the Elector Palatine, who married the daughter of our James the First. During the latter period he visited this country, and was employed by Henry, Prince of Wales, in ornamenting the gardens of Richmond Palace. The passage referred to by M. Arago is very much as follows :— Let there be attached to a ball of copper, *a*, a tube, *b*, and stop-cock, *c*, and also another tube, *d*; these tubes should reach almost to the bottom of the copper ball, and be well soldered in every part. The copper ball should then be filled with water through the tube *b*, and the stop-cock be shut, when, if the ball is placed on a fire, the heat acting upon it will cause the water to rise in the tube *d*, as indicated in the engraving.

A few years after the appearance of De Caus's work, an Italian engineer, named Giovanni Branca, published a book wherein he pointed out numerous novel applications to which steam power might be directed. The machine he proposed using consisted of a wheel with flat vanes upon its rim, similar to the boards of a paddle-wheel. The steam was to have been produced in a close vessel and made to issue with considerable force out of a tube directed against the vanes, which would cause the revolution of the wheel. Unlike some of the inventions we have previously enumerated, this method of Branca's bears no resemblance whatever to any application of steam power in use in engines of the present day.

We come now to a more interesting portion of our narrative, inasmuch as the claims of one of our own countrymen, namely, the Marquis of Worcester, to the honour of being regarded as one of the chief inventors of the steam-engine, will engage our attention. The Marquis of Worcester, living in the exciting times of the civil wars between Charles the First and his parliament, took part with the king, and after losing all his fortune in the cause was imprisoned in Ireland by his adversaries. He managed however to escape, and hastened over to France, whence after spending some time at the court of the exiled royal family of England, he returned to this country as their secret agent, but being detected, was confined a prisoner in the Tower. It is said that during this imprisonment, while he was engaged one day in cooking his own dinner, he observed the lid of the pot was continually being forced upwards by the vapour of the boiling water contained in the vessel. Being a

11

man of thoughtful disposition, and having, moreover, a taste for scientific investigation, he began to reflect on the circumstance, when it occurred to him that the same power which was capable of raising the iron cover of the pot might be applied to a variety of useful purposes; and on obtaining his liberty, he set to work to produce a practical exposition of his ideas on the subject in the shape of an acting machine, which he described in his work in the following terms :—

" I have invented an admirable and forcible way to drive up water by fire; not by drawing or sucking it upwards, for that must be, as the philosopher terms it, *intra sphæram activitatis*, which is but at such a distance. But this way hath no bounder if the vessels be strong enough. For I have taken a piece of whole cannon whereof the end was burst, and filled it three-quarters full of water, stopping and screwing up the broken end, as also the touch-hole, and making a constant fire under it; within twenty-four hours, it burst and made a great crack. So that, having a way to make my vessels so that they are strengthened by the force within them, and the one to fill after the other, I have seen the water run like a constant fountain stream forty feet high. One vessel of water rarified by fire driveth up forty of cold water, and a man that tends the work has but to turn two cocks; that one vessel of water being consumed, another begins to force and refill with cold water, and so successively; the fire being tended and kept constant, which the self-same person may likewise abundantly perform in the interim between the necessity of turning the said cocks."

In the accompanying figure of the Marquis of Worcester's engine it represents the boiler composed of arched iron plates, with their convex sides turned inward; they are fastened at the joinings by bolts passing through holes in their sides, which also pass through the ends of the rods i, i, i, a series of which rods extend from end to end of the boiler, being a few inches

12

apart. The ends of the boiler are hemispherical, and are fastened to flanges on the plates *h, h, h.* It will be evident

that each plate being an arch, before the boiler can burst, several, if not nearly all the rods *i, i, i,* must either be pulled asunder or torn from the bolts at the point of junction; and as the strength of the rods and bolts may be increased to any extent without interrupting the action of the fire, there can be no doubt that a boiler might be so constructed as to be perfectly safe under any pressure which could be required for raising water in a given height, because the pressure in such a boiler will never exceed the weight of a column of water equal in height to the cistern; *b, c* represent two vessels which communicate with the boiler *a,* by means of the pipes *f, f,* and the way-cocks *m, n,* and with the reservoir from which the water is to be drawn by the pipes *l, l; g, g,* are two tubes, through which the water is elevated to the cistern, they reach nearly to the bottom of the vessels *b, c,* and are open at each end. The pipe *l,* as well as *f, f,* communicate with the vessels *b, c,* by means of the way-cocks *m, n,* which, by moving the handles *o, p,* can be so placed that either the steam from the boiler, or the water from the reservoir, shall instantly have access to the

13

vessels *b, c.* Fire having been kindled under the boiler *a*, in the furnace *d*, the cock *n* is placed in the position represented in the drawing, when the water will have free access from the reservoir to the vessel *c*, which being filled, the handle *p* is turned back, so that the cock shall be relatively in the position shown at *m*; the steam then fairly enters through the pipe *f* into the vessel *c*, and having no other mode of escape presses on the surface of the water, which it forces up through the pipe *g*. During this operation, the pipe *m* having been placed as shown at *n*, the vessel *b* is filling from the reservoir through the pipe *l*, so that the water in the vessel *c* being consumed, the handle *o* of the cock *m* is turned, which admits the steam on the surface of the water in *b*, shutting off by the same operation the communication between *b* and the reservoir.

In considering the claims of the Marquis of Worcester to be regarded as *the* inventor of the steam-engine, the young reader must bear in mind that although the latest of the various treatises in reference to the moving power of steam, to which we have already alluded, had been printed some time previous to the appearance of any notification of the Marquis of Worcester's discovery, in all probability he had never seen or heard of any one of these works; for books in those days were in comparatively little request, and beyond editions of the Classics and of works of a purely religious character, very few books printed abroad, except such as had excited extraordinary attention on the Continent, were introduced into this country. Works, too, of a scientific tendency, were the least likely of all to find their way over here, for in spite of the impetus given to it by Bacon, and of the grand discoveries of Harvey (who, it will be recollected, first called attention to the circulation of the blood), the study of philosophical matters was yet in its earliest infancy. Such studies would, moreover, have been for the most part neglected, when the stirring incidents of a protracted civil war were, day by day, engaging men's attention. In addition to

14

all these circumstances, it should be recollected that the knowledge of continental languages was very limited, and unlike the
present age, which sends forth its translations in every European
language of works of mediocre character, no foreign work, except
those of the very highest reputation, was rendered into the
English tongue.

It should, however, be stated that the French people assert
that the Marquis of Worcester took the idea of the steam-
engine from De Caus, and in proof of this assertion bring
forward a letter from Marian Delorme, a celebrated beauty of
the reign of Louis the Thirteenth, to M. Cinq Mars, beheaded
by order of Cardinal Richelieu for the part taken by him in
some conspiracy. This letter, which, if it be genuine, certainly
proves that the Marquis of Worcester was acquainted with De
Caus's invention, is as follows :—

" 3rd February, 1641.

" Whilst you forget me at Narbonne, where you give your-
self up to the pleasures of the court, and delight in vexing
my Lord Cardinal, I, in accordance with the wish you
expressed to me, do the honours at Paris to your great English
lord, the Marquis of Worcester, and I escort him, or rather he
escorts me, from one curious sight to another ; for example,
we paid a visit to Bicêtre, where he pretends, in a madman, to
have discovered a man of genius ! Whilst crossing the court
yard of the hospital, more dead than alive from fear, and
clinging to my companion, an ugly countenance presented
itself behind the large iron bars, and cried loudly, ' I am not
mad ! I have made a discovery which must enrich any
country that will put it operation.' ' And, pray, what is his
discovery ?' said I to the keeper who showed us the establishment. ' Ah !' replied he, shrugging his shoulders, ' something very simple, but that you would never guess. It 's the
application of boiling water.' I burst out laughing. ' This
man,' continued the keeper, ' calls himself Solomon De Caus ;

15

he came from Normandy four years ago to present to the king a treatise upon the wonderful effects of steam. Cardinal Richelieu dismissed this madman without hearing him. Solomon De Caus, instead of being discouraged, followed my lord the Cardinal everywhere, who, annoyed at finding him continually crossing his path and importuning him with his follies, ordered his imprisonment at Bicêtre, where he has been for three years and a half. He cries out to every stranger that he is not a madman, and that he has made an admirable discovery.' 'Conduct me near to him,' said Lord Worcester; 'I wish to speak with him.' They conducted his lordship, but he returned sad and thoughtful. 'Now,' he exclaimed, 'he is indeed mad; misfortune and captivity have for ever injured his reason. You have made him mad; for when you cast him into this dungeon you cast there the greatest genius of his time, and in my country, instead of being imprisoned, he would have been loaded with riches.'"

. The occurrence above narrated, if true, must have taken place during the sojourn of the Marquis of Worcester in France after his flight from Ireland, where, as before mentioned, he had been imprisoned for the support rendered by him to the cause of Charles the First.

In reference to the invention of the Marquis of Worcester, Dr. Lardner observes, that "on comparing it with the contrivance previously suggested by De Caus, it will be observed, that even if De Caus knew the physical agent by which the water was driven upwards in the apparatus described by him, still it was only a method of causing a vessel of boiling water to empty itself; and before a repetition of the process could be made, the vessel should be refilled, and again boiled. In the contrivance of Lord Worcester, on the other hand, the agency of the steam was employed in the same manner as it is in the steam-engines of the present day, being generated in one vessel and used for mechanical purposes in another. Nor

16

must this distinction be regarded as trifling or insignificant, because on it depends the whole practicability of using steam as a mechanical agent. Had its action been confined to the vessel in which it was produced, it never could have been employed for any useful purpose."

We are indebted to a French philosopher named Papin for the discovery of the idea of producing a moving power by means of a piston working in a cylinder, to be effected by the condensation of the steam into water. We have already mentioned that a pint of water when converted into steam swells to the extraordinary amount of two hundred and sixteen gallons, filling somewhere about seventeen hundred times more space than it occupied in its liquid form. Of course when this steam is reconverted into water, it subsides again into its former dimensions. Papin's plan was, after having raised the piston by the elastic force of the steam beneath it which filled the cylinder, to condense this steam into water and thereby create a vacuum; on this being accomplished, the piston was pressed down again by the force of the atmosphere above. Papin constructed a small model, showing that this was to be effected, but beyond this no further steps were taken by him to carry out his important discovery.

After the lapse of some few years, the necessities of the mining operations in Cornwall at length drew the attention of the practical men there engaged to some means of drawing off the water which continually accumulated in the mines; and Captain Thomas Savery, in the year 1698, devised a machine for that purpose. This was a combination of the machine suggested by the Marquis of Worcester with an apparatus for raising water by suction into a vacuum produced by the condensation of steam. Savery, however, appeared to have been ignorant of Papin's discovery, for he stated that he derived the idea of his machine from the following circumstances:—Having drank a flask of Florence at a tavern, he flung the flask on the fire, and called for a basin of water to wash his hands. A small quantity of the wine that remained in the flask began to boil, and steam issued from its mouth; it occurred to him to try what effect would be produced by inverting the flask and plunging its mouth into cold water. Putting on a thick glove to defend his hand from the heat, he seized the flask, and the moment he plunged its mouth into water, the liquid rushed into the flask and filled it.

Reasoning upon the foregoing circumstance, Savery came to the conclusion that instead of exhausting the barrel of the pump by the usual laborious method of a piston and sucker, it might be accomplished by first filling it with steam and then condensing the steam when the atmospheric pressure would force the water from the mine into the pump barrel, and thence into any vessel connected with it, provided the vessel was not more than thirty-four feet above the level of water in the mine. He thought, after having raised the water to this height, that he might use the elastic force of steam at a high temperature to lift the water to a much greater elevation, after the plan proposed by the Marquis of Worcester, and by condensing this same steam, he considered he could reproduce the vacuum and thereby draw up more water. Savery's machine may be described as follows :—

The engine was fixed in a good double furnace, so contrived that the flame of the fire might circulate round and encompass the boilers Before the fire was lighted, the two small gauge-pipes and cocks G and N belonging to the two boilers were unscrewed, and the larger boiler L filled two-thirds full of water, and the small boiler D quite full. The said pipes were then screwed on again, as fast and as tight as possible. The fire b was then lighted, and when the water boiled in the large boiler the cock of the vessel P (shown in section) was opened. This made the steam rising from the water in L pass with irresistible force through O into P, pushing

13

out all the air before it through the clack R. When the air had left the vessel, the bottom of it became very hot; the cock

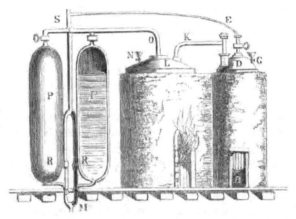

of the pipe of this vessel was then shut, and the cock of the other vessel P opened until that vessel had discharged its air through the clack R up the force-pipe s. In the mean time, a stream of cold water (supplied by a pipe connected with the discharging pipe s, but not shown in the cut) was passed over the outside of the vessel P, which, by condensing the steam within, created a vacuum, and the water from the well necessarily rose up through the sucking pump (cut off below M), lifting up the clack M, and filling the vessel P.

The first vessel P being emptied of its air, the cock was again opened, when the force of steam from the boiler pressed upon the surface of the water with an elastic quality like air, still increasing in elasticity, or spring, till it counterpoised or rather exceeded the weight of water ascending in the pipe s, out of which the water was immediately discharged when it had once reached the top.

The woodcut represents two reservoirs P P, designed for alternate action; the tube E was for the purpose of conveying water from the discharging pipe, to replenish the boiler L when the water in it began to get consumed; this was done by keeping the boiler D supplied with water, and by lighting the fire at B generating a sufficiency of steam to press the water into L, through the pipe K.

This was in reality the germ of the steam-engine as we now have it, and the principle is plainly perceptible through all the changes and manifold improvements of later days; but it was not until the alterations made by Newcomen, who was also a Cornish agent, in 1705, that it was brought into any extensive or effective use. This, however, may be called rather an atmospheric than a steam-engine, although it was the grand connecting link between the old plan and the complete machine as afterwards improved by the hands of the immortal James Watt.

In Newcomen's engine there was a cylinder c open at the upper end, through which a piston h worked. This end of the piston was fastened to a beam i resting at the middle on a pier or shaft, and weighed at both ends by a curved piece of iron, something like a small portion of the rim of a wheel, in order to give a greater effect to the pump with which this beam was connected at the other end. At the lower part of the cylinder there was a chamber, which, by means of a steam-pipe e, communicated with a boiler a. In order to preserve it air-tight, the upper part of the cylinder was kept about six inches deep in water. On each side, at the bottom of the cylinder, there was a cock—one communicating with a reservoir of water g, and which when opened allowed a jet of water to enter the cylinder through the pipe d; another, which allowed the condensed steam and air to escape through f down the pipe o. In the accompanying diagram of New-comen's engine, the interior of the lower part of the cylinder is shown for the purpose of representing this portion of the machine. The safety-valve b was raised when the steam

20

produced by the boiler exceeded the pressure of the atmosphere by more than one pound on the square inch, and the

steam escaped through it. The water being boiling, the cock *k* in the steam-pipe *e* was opened by the attendant, who pushed down the handle to *j*; this gradually filled the lower part of the cylinder with steam, but the power of the steam being only sufficient to equal the pressure of the atmosphere, would not of itself raise the piston and beam; this was therefore effected by means of the weight or counterpoise *l*, and the elevation of the piston forced down the pump rod *m* into the pump below. The attendant then returned the handle to its original position, which prevented the admission of more steam

21

from the boiler, and at the same time opened the cock *n*, which, communicating with the reservoir *g*, threw a jet of cold water into the cylinder. This instantly condensed the steam, and the piston, as it descended, in consequence of the pressure of the super-incumbent atmosphere, drove out the water and air from the bottom of the cylinder, and raised the pump-bucket in the mine. The steam-cock was again opened, and the piston again rose; again the steam was condensed, the piston descended, the water and air were driven out, and so the process went on so long as the services of the engine were required.

Humphrey Potter, a mere lad, who was occupied in attending to the cocks of an atmospheric engine, becoming anxious to escape from the monotonous drudgery imposed upon him, ingeniously contrived the adjustment of a number of strings, which, being attached to the beam of the engine, opened and closed the cocks with the most perfect regularity and certainty as the beam moved upwards and downwards, thus rendering the machine totally independent of manual superintendence. The contrivance of Potter was soon improved upon, and the whole apparatus was subsequently, about the year 1718, brought into complete working order by an engineer named Beighton.

Newcomen's engine, improved in several ways by Brindley, Smeaton, and other engineers, continued in use during the greater part of the last century; but it continued, in effect, the same until the days of Watt, and was almost entirely employed in the pumping of water. Watt's first improvement was an alteration of the mode of condensing the steam. Instead of using the method which has just been described, he had a condenser attached to the cylinder, and he still further improved upon it by surrounding his condenser with a tank of cold water, which was drawn from an adjoining well or reservoir by the pump of the engine.

Another improvement effected in the steam-engine, was

22

the custom adopted by Watt, of closing the top of the cylinder, the piston being made to work through a sort of neck, called a *stuffing-box*, which was rendered steam-tight by being lined with tow saturated with grease, which rubbed and greased the rod, and made it move easily.

By this alteration the elastic force of the steam was used as it is now, to impel the piston downwards as well as upwards. But, as yet, no means had been provided to enable the piston to move upwards as well as downwards; and when it had reached the bottom, the counterpoise at the pump-rod raised it again. To obviate this defect, Watt contrived a means by which the steam, after having served its purpose, was allowed to go under the piston, and to pass thence into the condenser, through a passage opened at the proper moment—something on the plan devised by the boy Potter. Such is the method still continued to the present time.

This only proves how great may be the results from the most trifling actions—if there be such a thing as a "trifle" in the world, while effects similar to this are continually arising from the most insignificant causes. The machine hence became a *steam-engine* instead of an atmospheric one, and all that continuous action from which so much benefit has been enjoyed was attained by this simple device.

James Watt, who was born at Greenock, in Scotland, in 1736, had, from his birth, an extremely delicate constitution. Being, as he grew up, too sickly to have those educational restraints imposed upon him to which youth are necessarily subjected, he was for the most part left at liberty to choose his own occupations and amusements. In the valuable work of Dr. Lardner, before quoted, the following anecdotes are told, showing the use made by young Watt of the freedom allowed him :—

"A friend of his father found the boy one day stretched upon the hearth tracing with chalk various lines and angles. 'Why do you permit this child,' said he, 'to waste his time so; why not send him to school?' Mr. Watt replied, 'You judge him hastily; before you condemn us ascertain how he is employed.' On examining the boy, then six years of age, it was found that he was engaged in the solution of a problem of Euclid!

"Having observed the tendency of his son's mind, Mr. Watt placed at his disposal a collection of tools. These he soon learned to use with the greatest skill. He took to pieces and put together, again and again, all the children's toys which he could procure; and he was constantly employed in making new ones. Subsequently he used his tools in constructing a little electrical machine, the sparks proceeding from which, became a great subject of amusement to all the playfellows of the poor invalid.

"Though endowed with great retentive powers, Watt would probably never have figured among the prodigies of a common school: he would have been slow to commit his lessons to memory, from the repugnance which he would feel to repeat like a parrot anything which he did not perfectly understand. The natural tendency of his mind to meditate on whatever came before it, would give him, to superficial observers, the appearance of dulness. Happily, however, he had a parent who was sufficiently clear-sighted, and who entertained high hopes of the growing faculties of his son. More distant and less sagacious relations were not so sanguine. One day Mrs. Muirhead, the aunt of the boy, reproaching him for what she conceived to be listless idleness, desired him to take a book and occupy himself usefully. 'More than an hour has now passed away,' said she, 'and you have not uttered a single word. Do you know what you have been doing all this time? You have taken off, and put on, repeatedly, the lid of the tea-pot; you have been holding the saucers and the spoons over the steam, and you have been endeavouring to catch the

24

drops of water formed on them by the vapour. Is it not a shame for you to waste your time so?'

"Mrs. Muirhead was little aware that this was the first experiment in the splendid career of discovery which was subsequently to immortalise her little nephew. She did not see, as we now can, in the little boy playing with the tea-pot, the great engineer preluding to those discoveries which were destined to confer on mankind benefits so inestimable."

At the age of nineteen, Watt was apprenticed for three years to Mr. Morgan, a mathematical instrument maker in Finch Lane, Cornhill. He remained with him, however, not more than a twelvemonth, when he returned to Glasgow, and shortly afterwards obtained the appointment of mathematical instrument maker to the university. At this time he numbered among his friends and patrons Adam Smith, the celebrated political economist, and other men celebrated for their scientific attainments, and his shop became a common rendezvous for both professors and students. Among the latter was one named Robinson, who afterwards distinguished himself by the production of various scientific works, which still hold a high place in this department of literature, and between him and Watt a lasting personal friendship was at this period formed. Robinson thus describes one of the most interesting traits of his friend's character :—

"I had always, from my earliest youth, a great relish for the natural sciences, and particularly for mathematical and mechanical philosophy, when I was introduced by Drs. Simson, Dick, and Moor, gentlemen eminent for their mathematical abilities, to Mr. Watt. I saw a workman, and expected no more ; but was surprised to find a philosopher as young as myself, and always ready to instruct me. I had the vanity to think myself a pretty good proficient in my favourite study, and was rather mortified at finding Mr. Watt so much my superior. . . . . Whenever any puzzle came in the way of any of the young students, we went to Mr. Watt. He needed only to be prompted, for everything became to him the beginning of a new and serious study, and we knew that he would not quit it till he had either discovered its insignificancy, or had made something of it.

. "When to his superiority of knowledge is added the *naïve* simplicity and candour of Mr. Watt's character, it is no wonder that the attachment of his acquaintances was strong. I have seen something of the world, and am obliged to say I never saw such another instance of general and cordial attachment to a person whom all acknowledged to be their superior."

It was about the year 1762, or 1763, that Watt's attention appears to have been first turned to the principle of the steam-engine, when he tried several experiments with what was called *Papin's Digester ;* and by balancing a piston-rod with a weight at one end, and then admitting steam under it, he succeeded in obtaining a continuous motion. But it was not until the following year that his inventive and acute faculties were truly practically engaged on the theme by which his great fame was obtained. There was in the college an old model of a steam-engine by Newcomen, which was constantly used to illustrate the lectures of the professors. It had got out of order—indeed it had never acted properly, and Watt, whose ingenuity appears at that time to have been highly appreciated, was employed to put it into working condition. He did so, most satisfactorily; but the business did not rest there. His sagacious mind soon perceived that the ill-working of Newcomen's machine was owing to its demanding two almost irreconcilable conditions—the requirement of water at a high temperature; and a perfect vacuum, which could only be obtained by an injection of cold water, which had the effect of lowering the temperature of the steam on its coming in contact with the sides of the cylinder and piston, after these had been cooled by the introduction of the cold water. This discovery laid the foundation of his plan for a separate condenser, which he afterwards carried out so successfully. By the middle of the year 1765, his invention was completed; and the effect of it was that a great saving was effected in the cost of fuel, as it did away with a large amount of wasteful expenditure of steam power. During the progress of this invention, however, one great anomaly struck him—for he found that steam of only 47 or 48 degrees of heat was sufficient to make water rise to the boiling heat of 212 of Farenheit's thermometer. On mentioning this strange circumstance to Dr. Black, that scientific person immediately showed him the cause of it, and then developed the qualities of latent heat, which he had lately discovered. Another great improvement introduced by Watt was the employment of steam instead of atmospheric air, to drive down the piston to the bottom of the cylinder. This was effected by letting the steam from the boiler enter above and below the piston alternately—the vacuum below the piston being also produced by the property of steam. Three years

27

elapsed from the time when these great discoveries were made by Watt before an opportunity was allowed him of carrying them into effect, on a sufficiently large scale to prove their working capabilities. This was at length accomplished by his introduction to Dr. Roebuck, when, after some negociations, a patent was taken out, and a partnership formed, Watt agreeing to cede to Roebuck two-thirds of all advantages to be derived from the invention. An experimental engine on a large scale was next constructed, the success of which, with the exception of a few practical difficulties that presented themselves, was most complete.

A few years afterwards Dr. Roebuck became embarrassed in his circumstances, and in 1773 a partnership was entered into by Watt with Mr. Matthew Boulton of Soho, near Birmingham, in

SOHO IRON WORKS

whose extensive establishment he found that assistance from able artizans and extensive capital which his most ardent wishes could desire. In the following year an application was made to Parliament for an extension of the patent, and in

28

1775 an Act was passed extending the term, which, according to the original patent, would have expired in 1783, for a period of seventeen years longer. Watt now applied himself vigorously to the perfection of his invention in all its practical details, and the result was the construction, on a large scale, of what is now known as his single acting steam-engine.

During the progress of those numerous minor improvements in the steam-engine which were continually being effected by Watt, one of the most interesting of which was that ingenious mechanical combination known as the parallel motion, he attempted to remedy the irregularity of action caused by the suspension of the power of the engine during the ascent of the piston rod; but while occupied in making various experiments, a workman in Watt's employ communicated the nature of the means by which Watt sought to effect the object in view to a person of the name of Wasborough, who at once adopted it, and took out a patent for the application of the crank to steam-engines.

To avoid litigation, Watt abandoned his idea of using a crank, and substituted for it a contrivance known as the sun and planet wheel. Neither of these inventions, however, served to maintain a regular rotatory motion such as was desired; but this was afterwards effected by means of a fly-wheel.

To remedy the irregularity of motion, produced by the unequal supply of steam from the boiler, Watt invented the throttle-valve, which, being placed in the pipe through which the steam is conveyed from the boiler to the cylinder, the opening and partial closing of it, by means of a lever, increased or reduced the supply of steam, according as it was required.

It being necessary that this lever should be moved by the man in charge of the engine, Watt foresaw that any want of proper vigilance and skill on his part would render the throttle-valve ineffectual for the uses to which it was designed.

He therefore connected the lever, by means of which its motions were regulated, with an apparatus, founded on the principle of the regulator employed in windmills, to which he gave the name of the governor. This had the effect of enabling the engineer at all times to regulate the monster of motion under his care to such a nicety, that although there is the power of some millions of horses now continually engaged, an accident is an infrequent occurrence. Such a degree of security, indeed, has been obtained, that it is said to be by no means uncommon, on the presence of visitors, for the director of an engine at the Cornish mines, where the most powerful machines in the world are employed, to step on the valve of his vast machine and stop it, until, perhaps, if checked one moment longer, it would blow him and all around into ten thousand atoms—a foolish feat which no one with a proper regard to the lives of others would venture to put in practice.

Before proceeding further with our history, we think it desirable to bring before the reader at one view the high state of perfection to which the steam-engine had been advanced by the superior intelligence and energy of Watt, that the reader may see how the many beautiful contrivances, emanating from the master mind of this greatest among mechanicians, when brought together, form one complete and harmonious whole. This object will, we think, be effected by the study of the diagram and description of the double-acting steam-engine here given.

The steam from the boiler is conveyed to the cylinder A through the steam-pipe B, the supply being regulated by the throttle-valve c, which valve is under the direct influence of the governor D. On one side of the cylinder, at the upper and lower ends, are attached two square hollow boxes, marked E, which communicate with the cylinder by means of a passage in the middle of each. These boxes have each two valves, by means of which they are divided into three compartments.

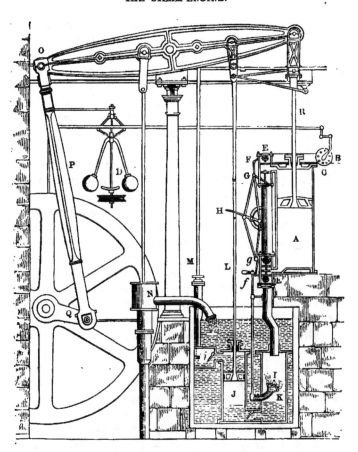

The top compartment in both boxes communicates with the steam-pipe, and the lower one with the eduction-pipe leading to the condenser. These valves move in pairs—that is, the upper induction-valve F and the lower exhaustion-valve f move together, and the same with the upper exhaustion-valve G and the lower induction-valve g. The piston R, being accurately fitted to the cylinder by packing, as it moves, divides the cylinder into two compartments, between which there is no communication. By opening the valve F, therefore, steam is admitted above the piston, while it is, at the same time, withdrawn from below the piston, and allowed to pass to the condenser by the opening of the valve f. In the same manner steam is withdrawn from above the piston by means of the valve G, and admitted beneath the piston through the valve g. These valves are all worked with one lever H (called the spanner), as will be shortly explained. Below the cylinder is the condensing apparatus, consisting of two cylinders, I and J, immersed in a cistern of cold water. A pipe K, having an end like the rose of a watering-pot, conveys water from the cistern to the cylinder I, the supply, which is, however, continual, being regulated by a cock. By this means the steam constantly passing into the cylinder I becomes condensed. The other cylinder J, called the air-pump, has a close-packed piston L, with valve in it opening upwards, which operates like the bucket of a common pump, and draws off the surplus water that is continually collecting at the bottom of the condenser I (through the passage which communicates between the two vessels at the lower part, by means of a valve opening towards the air-pump) into the upper reservoir j. The hot water pump M then conveys this water into the tank which supplies the boiler. The cold water pump N supplies the cistern, in which the air-pump and condenser are submerged, so as to keep down its temperature to the proper limit. On the rod of the air-pump two pins are placed so as to strike the spanner H upwards and downwards at the proper times when the piston approaches the termination of the stroke at the top or bottom of the cylinder. To the working end of the beam O a rod of cast iron P, called the connecting rod, is attached, and which is again fixed at its other end to the crank Q, by means of a pivot. Its weight is such that it serves to balance the

32

weight of the piston-rod, of the air-pump and cylinder on the other side of the beam; while the weight of the rod of the cold water pump is nearly equivalent to that of the rod of the hot water pump. On the axle of the crank is placed the fly-wheel, and connected with it is the governor D, which regulates the throttle-valve, as before mentioned.

The working of the engine is as follows:—Supposing the piston to be at the top of the cylinder, and the whole of the space below to be filled with steam, the upper steam-valve and the lower exhausting-valve will be opened by the spanner being raised by the lower pin of the air-pump rod, while the upper exhausting-valve and the lower steam-valve are closed. By this means steam will be admitted above the piston, and the steam beneath it be drawn off into the condenser, where it will be converted into water. The effect of this will be the forcing of the piston, by the pressure of the steam above it, to the bottom of the cylinder. Just as this takes place, the spanner will be moved downwards by the upper pin on the rod of the air-pump, and the valves that were previously opened closed, while those that remained closed will be, at the same time, opened. The steam will, therefore, be admitted into the cylinder beneath the piston, and the steam above be drawn off into the condenser, and be converted into water as before. While the above action is going on, the air-pump will draw off the hot water in the condenser into the upper reservoir, and, at the same time, the hot water pump will convey this water back again to the tank which supplies the boiler.

Several years elapsed before the parties connected with the mining interests were disposed to take any notice of the great advantages which were pointed out as certain to result to them from the employment of engines possessing these vast improvements. The one great advantage which, as commercial men, they ought readily to have appreciated, was the enormous saving that might be effected in fuel. In the

most improved forms which the atmospheric engine invented by
Savery had at that time attained, as much steam was wasted at
every stroke of the piston as sufficed to fill the cylinder, consequently as much was wasted as was beneficially employed;
while in Watt's engines the waste was only one quarter of the
contents of the cylinder. Another advantage of the improved
engine was to be found in the fact that it would work under a
pressure of ten pounds on the square inch, which was three
pounds more than the atmospheric engine could accomplish
under the same circumstances. Notwithstanding these important advantages, Watt and Boulton were compelled to make
large sacrifices to bring their engines into use, as will be seen
by the following proposition, submitted at the time to the
Carron Company by Mr. Boulton:—

"We have no objection," he writes, " to contract with you
to direct the making of an engine to return the water to your
mills. We do not aim at profits in engine-building, but shall
take our profits out of the saving of fuel; so that if we save
nothing, we shall take nothing. Our terms are as follows:
we will make all the necessary plans, sections, and elevations
for the building, and for the engine with its appurtenances,
specifying all cast and forged iron work, and every other
particular relative to the engine. We will give all necessary
directions to your workmen, which they must implicitly obey.
We will execute, for a stipulated price, the valves, and all
other parts which may require exact execution, at Soho; we
will see that all the parts are put together, and set to work,
properly; we will keep our own work in repair for one year,
and we have no other objection to seven years than the
nconvenience of the distance. We will guarantee that the
engine so constructed shall raise at least 20,000 cubic feet
of water twenty-four feet high with each hundredweight of
coals burnt.

"When all this is done, a fair and candid comparison

shall be made between it, and your own engine or any other engine in Scotland, from which comparison the amount of savings in fuel shall be estimated, and that amount being divided into three parts, we shall be entitled to one of those parts, in recompense for our patent licence, our drawings, &c. &c. Our own share of savings shall be estimated in money, according to the value of your coals delivered under the boiler, and you shall annually pay us that sum, during twenty-five years from the day you begin to work; provided you continue the use of the engine so long. And in case you sell the engine, or remove it to any other place, you must previously give us notice, for we shall then be entitled to our third of the savings of fuel, according to the value of coals at such new place. This is a necessary condition, otherwise the engine which we make for you at an expense of £2,000 may be sold in Cornwall for £10,000.

" Such parts of the engine as we execute at Soho we will be paid for at a fair price; I conclude, from all the observations I have had the opportunity of making, that our engines are four times better than the common engines. In boilers, which are a very expensive article, the savings will be in proportion to the savings of coal. If you compare our engine with the common engine (not in size, but in power), you will find the original expense of erecting one to be nearly the same."

The patent right which had been granted to Boulton and Watt for their improved engine having expired in the year 1800, Watt retired altogether from the firm, leaving his two sons (one of whom, however, died a few years afterwards), in conjunction with his former partner, to reap the benefits certain to result from those successful efforts of his genius which had, step by step, brought the steam-engine to its then state of perfection. Watt resided at this time on his own estate of Heathfield, in Staffordshire, enjoying the friendship of a large circle of friends, by whom his amiable qualities were appreciated as they deserved to be, and, as may be imagined, still devoting his time to intellectual pursuits.

HEATHFIELD HOUSE.

Previous to this time, in the mining districts of Cornwall the new engines had replaced the old ones, and in order to ascertain the saving effected by them without the unpleasantness of having a person commonly on the premises to exercise what might be felt to be a prying inspection, Watt invented an apparatus for counting and registering the strokes made by the great beam of the engine, and thus ascertaining the duty it had performed. This apparatus was deposited in a box to which there were two keys; one of these was left with the proprietor of the engine, and the other was kept by a confidential agent of the patentees, who opened the register once every three months, in the presence of the proprietors, to ascertain the rent that was due. The advantage of the saving of fuel was constant, and, shortly afterwards, the several proprietors readily assented to pay an annual sum to the patentees in lieu of this varying charge; and some idea may be formed of the immense advantage of the improved engine to the public, and of the reward obtained by the inventors, when it is stated that in one instance alone the lessees of Chacewater Mine, in Cornwall, paid £800 a-year as a rent-charge for each of the three large engines which they kept at work.

STATUE OF WATT, BY CHANTREY, IN HANDSWORTH CHURCH.

HINDOO WEAVER.

THE COTTON MANUFACTURE.

HE progress of a nation shows itself as much in the improvement of dress as it does in any other of the arts which tend to civilize life. If we turn to the England of two thousand years ago, we find the inhabitants clothed in skins, and the chiefs wearing only a coarse kind of cloth but little better than common sacking. Even the mailed knight, who makes such a figure in the age of chivalry, when divested of his shining armour, often wore only a leathern doublet, unless on state occasions, when the ermined tunic and embroidered vest, on which his arms were emblazoned, were put on, more to swell the heraldic pomp than for either warmth or comfort.

For ages after our grandmothers sat down to the spinning-wheel, and spun the yarn which was afterwards sent to the weaver and woven into those strong homely dresses which were bequeathed from mother to daughter through generations. There were not in those primitive ages drapers' shops in every town and village, as there are now—only the chapman, or pedlar, who came round at certain periods with his pack-horse, sometimes supplying the little shopkeeper, but oftener calling from house to house, as the hawkers of Scotch and Irish linens do in the present day. As for Cotton, it was unknown in England until the last two centuries; for such goods as bore the name were made out of wool or flax: the "spinning-jenny" was never dreamed of—only the old "weaver's beam and shuttle," with very little improvement, the same as that mentioned in the Book of Job. What these ancient clothes were, may be seen by examining such as have been brought from the Theban tombs, or are swathed around the Egyptian mummies.

But our present is an inquiry into the rise and progress of the greatest English manufacture which machinery and steam have been brought to assist and impel, and after having briefly investigated it, our task will be to draw attention to inventions of the highest value connected with it, such as those ingenious and multiplex machines called "the spinning-jenny" and "the power-loom."

But few of the creations of inventive genius have tended more to enhance the prosperity, and increase the influence of a great people, than these instruments of multiplied labour. Intended, originally, simply to assist one of the useful arts, and that, according to the usual estimation of the world, not the most honourable among them, these machines have wrought a total change in the modes of trade and the extent of the manufactures of Britain; and it is not too much to assert, that that extent of empire which this country now possesses never could have been obtained, nor could the wealth necessary for its welfare and protection ever have been acquired, without their aid. Viewed in this light, the several inventions which have contributed to realize that immense amount of business which helps to feed and clothe many millions of human beings, become of importance in more than a mere mechanical point of view.

It is a remarkable fact that, while in the higher departments of machinery, where the principles of science properly so called have been requisite, as in the steam-engine and the electric telegraph, the moderns have created new fields for enterprise and new means for enjoyment, they have barely equalled and perhaps never surpassed the ancients in the construction of those articles which are formed by the exertions of the handicraft artizan. At all times clothing, to some extent at least, was necessary in the states where civilization existed to any, however small a degree, and we find in the antique monuments of Thebes plain representations of the implements by which the inhabitants wove the cloth that protected them from the changes or the inclemency of the weather.

Even at the present day, the Hindoo, seated on the ground, with his legs in a hole, and the weft of his muslin tied to the branches of a couple of trees, throws his shuttle with a skill that, in the end, produces the most beautiful muslin or calico ; but yet such is the superiority obtained by the use of machinery, that the cotton grown on his native plains can be brought ten thousand miles, cleansed, spun, woven, dried, packed, and carried back again, and then sold in the province where its woolly fibre first silvered the bud, at a less price than that of the cloth produced by the Indian artizan.

It is unnecessary to remark that cloth made by weaving is formed by interlacing the threads with each other crosswise, but it is not so generally known that there are regular terms for all the different kinds of weaving. Thus plain weaving is

40

merely the process of making each single thread interlace with that next to it, by means of a shuttle sent horizontally between the threads which are placed upright before the weaver. In weaving what are called twilled stuffs, the shuttle is made to pass over one and under two, or over two and under three or four, just as it is desired to produce that diagonal line which we perceive in galloons, bombazines, and all fabrics of similar manufacture. When stripes are to be produced, the colours are arranged in the warp, which is the name given to the long threads, while the weft, as the cross threads are called, is made to pass in the usual manner; but when checks are required, the colours have to be arranged both in the warp and weft; and in the weaving of all kinds of patterns they are produced by making the weft to pass under and over at particular spots, wherever it is wished that the spots or flowers should be seen. When that beautiful species of fabric is desired which we often see in silks, showing various beautiful hues as the light falls upon it, and which is termed "shot silk," the warp is of one colour and the weft of another.

In all probability the weft was in the first place formed by throwing a ball of thread through the *shed*, as that open space is called which is formed by the weaver treading down first one treddle and then the other, to raise or depress the alternate warp threads. And this ball, unwinding as it passed along, formed the weft; but afterwards a more convenient means was adopted in the common *shuttle*, which is a piece of wood something in the shape of a boat, hollowed out in the middle where the thread or cotton is placed, and so protected from the rubbing to which it would be otherwise subject. In the commonest modes of weaving the shuttle is passed from side to side with both hands; but about a hundred years ago what is termed the *fly-shuttle* was invented by an ingenious person of the name of Kay, who resided at Bury. By this invention the shuttle, with the aid of a string, can be

41

cast both ways by the same hand, so that the workman saves a considerable portion of his time in the operation.

In India and China, to the present day, the warp is formed by laying the threads side by side in an open field; and in the infancy of cotton manufacture in England, the same plan was commonly followed, but the uncertainty of the climate neces-. sarily subjected the process to frequent hindrance, and a machine was invented called the *warping-mill*. This consists of a number of upright posts which are fastened at top and bottom into the rim of a wheel, with a shaft which turns like an axle in the centre. This is made to revolve by means of what is called an endless rope—that is, a rope with the ends fastened together—which is passed round a little flat axis, and wound round and round by means of a handle. Close by this there is an upright framing, in which a number of bobbins are fixed, four or five end to end, and several tiers one above another. The ends of the threads of these several bobbins are then brought all together and passed through a sliding piece, which by means of a rope is made to travel up and down the outer framing of the mill. By turning the axis, therefore, the threads are made to wind spirally round the mill, and when a sufficient length has been obtained, by means of some pins the motion of the mill is reversed, and the process is thus continued until a sufficient number of threads has been obtained to form the whole breadth of the warp. This, then, is attached to the frame of the weaving machine, and the cross threads are interlaced as has been already described.

Calico, the fabric on which the produce of the cotton plant has been chiefly employed, obtained its name from *Calicat*, an insignificant town in the peninsula of India, where, from the most authentic records that we have, it was first made. On its first introduction into Britain it was an article too expensive to be purchased by the labouring classes; and it was little thought, in the early days of its manufacture, how wonderfully it was destined to alter the whole face of society. Originally that cloth which was known under the name of *calico* did not consist, as at present, entirely of *cotton*, but was composed of yarn formed from the fibres of flax for its long threads, or warp, and had cotton only for its cross ones, or weft. This was owing to the great difference between the strength of the threads of the former plant and those formed of the fruit of cotton.

If the filamentous portions of these two plants be cast into water, it will be perceived that those of flax are composed of long capillary threads of a woody texture, occasionally exhibiting longitudinal joints; while the hairs, for so they may be termed, of the cotton pod, look like thin flat ribbons either without any joints at all, or when they have any, with junctions cutting straight across the ribbon, the portions of which are of course easily divided from each other. The fibres of flax are also always intertwisted among each other in bundles requiring some little force to separate them, whereas those of cotton are almost invariably distinct, and are with difficulty brought to coalesce so as to form a continuous thread.

Respecting the number of species of the cotton plant there are various statements; 'some authors asserting that there are not more than eight, while others affirm that there are upwards of a hundred, and indeed that there is no end to them. Botanists have, unfortunately, never taken the trouble to cultivate a great variety of them, in order to ascertain precisely the difference between the several kinds. But attempts, nevertheless, have been made to do this to some extent by other parties, and those too under very favourable circumstances, for there have been gardens for the purpose in Jamaica, Trinidad, and St. Vincent's, where the various plants of the numerous regions where the cotton shrub is found have been grown side by side. But the garden in Trinidad alone remains, and it does not appear that any great advantage has arisen from that. Thus much, however, we know, that the several species differ materially in appearance, varying from four or five, to fifteen or sixteen feet high.

That the plant was well known in ancient times there is no doubt, but at what period it was introduced into the localities from which our supplies are now chiefly drawn, is not so precisely stated. The finest and best kind, which is known by the name of *Sea Island Cotton*, from its being grown on the low sandy islands off the coast of the United States, is the produce of a plant that appears to have been first carried to the Bahamas from the island of Anguilla (whither it is believed to have been transported from Persia), and was sent to Georgia in 1786. But there is evidence of the existence of the cotton plant in America long before there was any direct communication between the civilized world and the two great portions of that continent, and we have it positively stated that the Spaniards found calico a common article in the dress of the inhabitants when they conquered Mexico. In China it does not appear to have been employed to constitute articles of dress before the thirteenth century of the Christian era, when its cheapness, as compared with the silks and woollens of the country, brought it into extensive use. The filaments of the cotton pod are believed to have been employed in Spain for weaving cloth by the Moors, in the tenth century; but the repulsive feeling which existed on the part of the Mohammedans and the Christians towards each other, kept the knowledge of its manufacture for many ages from the rest of Europe. In this continent calico was first made in Italy, which, before the discovery of the passage to the East, by the Cape of Good Hope, was the great entrepôt of commerce between India and the West. But it was not until the spreading enterprise of Britain, and the genius of Arkwright, Hargreaves, and Cartwright, brought it into extensive use, that it was much esteemed as an article of utility.

The cotton used for manufacturing purposes is distinguished

44

by the length and shortness, the silkiness and coarseness, and the weakness and strength of the several filaments. These filaments are the downy hairs which grow on the surface of the white seed-pod of the cotton plant, and are particularly affected in their quality by the situation in which it is grown. Some species of the plant thrive best where they can have the benefit of the sea air, and the produce is fine in proportion to their nearness or distance from the coast. Others again require the interior of the country. In dry climates the best plants, as on the mountain-bound shores of Brazil, are met with on the coast; while in damp climates, like that of Pennambuco, the most valuable produce is obtained from the interior. But whether seen bordering the lofty acclivities of the Andes, with the wide Pacific heaving its boundless waves to a limitless horizon, beneath a sky of more than Italian azure, or met with in the broad rich valleys bright with the luxuriant bloom of tropical wild-flowers, a field of cotton shrubs, with their dark green leaves and silvery pods, with here and there a magnificent mangolia or a noble palm rearing its lofty head above its lower brethren, is at all times a beautiful sight, and more especially in the picking season, when hosts of busy labourers are gathering the valuable produce, and preparing it for shipment, to enrich and to comfort the inhabitants of distant climes.

Sea Island cotton is only found in Georgia, Florida, and South Carolina, and is often termed by the inhabitants of the Southern States "*black* seed cotton," from the seed contained in the pods being black, while the seeds of the short staple cotton, or that which has the short filaments, is called the "*green* seed cotton," for a similar reason. This latter kind is also called *bowed* Georgia or *upland* cotton, having acquired the latter appellation from its being grown in the upper districts of the state, instead of on the low tracts along the seacoast. It was called bowed cotton because the strings of a bow were made to twang sharply upon the mass of produce, and

45

thus, by repeated strokes, to loose the locks of cotton, in order to separate as far as possible the seeds from the filaments, the latter of course alone being serviceable for the manufacture of cloth; but this process is now more speedily and effectually accomplished by the use of a machine, invented by an American, called a *saw-gin*.

Having been made as free as possible from the seeds and from the soil upon it, the cotton, in its raw state, is packed in large bales and transmitted to other countries. Of that which is grown in all parts of the world, considerably more than half is sent to Great Britain, America and India each retaining a large portion of the remainder of their produce for their own use.

It is calculated that a return of from $4d.$ to $5d.$ per lb. will remunerate the grower for his outlay and give him a fair profit; and it is astonishing to observe how, through the unity of economy, exertion, and enterprise, the original cost of this great necessary of life has been reduced. By the official returns it appears that from 1791 to 1795, a period when the manufacture of cotton was beginning to expand to its subsequent immense extent, the average price of all the sorts of cotton was $15\frac{1}{2}d.$ per lb.; in the next five years, no supplies being received from America, in consequence of our hostilities with France, it rose to $18\frac{1}{2}d.$ per lb. In 1800 a treaty was entered into with the United States, one article of which provided that no goods previously imported by them from the West Indies should be exported in American vessels, and the shipment of cotton to this country in consequence of it became very large, and the price fell to $12\frac{1}{2}d.$; in the next five years it was $9\frac{1}{2}d.$, in the next $7\frac{1}{2}d.$, but from 1816 to 1820 it rose to $13d.$, chiefly from the great distress that prevailed through the bad harvests, and deficient trade during that time; but in the next five years it fell to $8d.$, and then to $5d.$, rising, however, to $6d.$ per lb. from 1831 to 1835; and that may now be stated as about the average price, though many entertain an opinion that it will be much reduced.

From land fresh brought under cultivation, in the best districts of America, the usual amount of produce is about 1000 lbs. weight per acre, which will yield about 300 lbs. of clean cotton, one able-bodied labourer being considered sufficient to cultivate eight acres of ground, when assisted by the aged, the infirm, and the young attached to the estate. When the ground has, however, been long brought under tillage, the produce is not expected to be much more than half this amount. In one of Captain Basil Hall's valuable works, he says that the whole number of negroes employed upon an estate of 200 acres was 122, of whom 48 were children, 4 too old to work; of the remaining 70, only 39 were considered "full hands," 16 were "three-quarter hands," 11 "half-hands," and 4 "quarter-hands;" the whole being equal to 57½ able-bodied labourers, who are allowed during their intervals of work opportunity for cultivating their own provision grounds. On the authority of Mr. Woodbury, one of the ministers of the United States, it is asserted that the whole quantity of ground occupied by the cotton plant is upwards of two millions of acres, and that there are upwards of a million persons engaged in the business of its cultivation, in that country alone.

The demand for cotton goods having been rising beyond the power of supply for a series of years, hope of profit impelled invention; and, among other contrivances, a machine was planned, and in 1738 a patent taken out for it, by Mr. Charles Wyatt of Birmingham, in the name of Lewis Paul, a foreigner with whom Wyatt was connected, and who was the principal inventor of the machine. Paul's plan was to spin the wool by means of several rollers; but it was ultimately abandoned, having been brought to no practical effect, although it was adduced when Arkwright, many years afterwards, endeavoured to bring his own invention into general use, as evidence that

47

he was not the first inventor. Perhaps not, but he was certainly the person who in the end brought the principle into common application. The intrinsic merits of the steam-engine as a motive agent must have been very apparent, for just at the time that James Watt was busily engaged in developing its merits and endeavouring to render it a perfect machine, and Mr. Miller of Dalswinton had glanced at it as a moving power, and Symington was intensely occupied in render-ing it applicable to general purposes, M. De Gennes published in the Philosophical Transactions—the date is 1768—an account of a machine to make linen cloth without the aid of an artificer. It was to be worked by water power, and the description con-tains all the germs of the power-loom which was thereafter to produce such wonderful results. The chief difficulty which he conceived he had to overcome was breaking the threads of the warp, and this he said his machine would obviate, by preventing the shuttle from touching them, while he averred that it would set ten or twelve looms at work, and the cloth might be made to any width. Yet this machine, ingenious as it was, never appears to have been of any practical use, and subsequently, Mr. Austin, Mr. Miller, and two Frenchmen, named respectively Dolignon and Vancanson, attempted the same thing. Of these, only that designed by Mr. Austin was brought to any practical effect, and a power-loom was put up by him in the factory of Mr. Monteith near Glasgow, but after a short time even this was laid aside. During the series of years throughout which the adaptation of the hand-loom to extensive manufacturing pur-poses was being brought about, an individual came into existence who was to do away with the great difficulty which had hitherto been felt, and who arrived at fame, fortune, and honour, through the exercise of his own implanted genius and energy, and under the blessing of that Providence without whose aid nothing truly valuable can ever be achieved.

Richard Arkwright was born of lowly parents in the town

of Preston, in the year 1732; his boyhood was passed in indigent circumstances, and he was at length apprenticed to a barber. After he had served his time he set up a business for himself in the neighbouring town of Bolton, where he continued to follow his humble occupation till he was twenty-eight years of age.

RICHARD ARKWRIGHT.

In 1760, he quitted his employment as a barber, and took to travelling up and down the country collecting hair, which he sold to the makers of wigs, who at that time had a business which, from the peculiar fashions of the time, was in great repute. This new business of Arkwright's is one still somewhat extensively followed on the continent with no small profit; and a curious instance of the way in which it is made available, is said to have occurred not long since in one of the western counties of England. A wag, with as much wit as he had little of honesty, made his appearance there, when a report of a violent epidemic in the country was very prevalent, and coolly issued a notice to the rustic inhabitants of the place and its neighbourhood, intimating that he was sent down by the Government to cut the hair of all the residents in the district, with a view to prevent the spread of. the cholera. As he had stated that his office was to be fulfilled free of expense, he had ,soon a numerous assemblage of patients, and quickly despoiled the country maidens of the luxuriant tresses with which nature had provided them. It is needless to observe that the quarantine agent had no commission from the Home Office, and that he doubtless made a very ample profit out of the rural credulity.

Certainly he had reason for a hearty laugh at the expense of those by whom he had been believed.

It is not to be supposed for a moment that Arkwright practised any such a trick as this for the improvement of his pecuniary resources; but it is stated that he possessed some peculiar secrets for dying hair, which greatly enhanced the value of the locks which he obtained from his customers. Whether he did possess such a secret seems somewhat doubtful, or at least discredit has been thrown upon the report, though it does not seem improbable, for the natural ingenuity of the man must have found vent in some shape or other.

His first efforts in mechanics were made to discover the "perpetual motion," which, from the time at which Arkwright was engaged upon it till the end of the first quarter of the present century, was a popular object of curiosity and expectation; there being a prevailing notion that Government would reward the discoverer of it with £10,000. Not long after his entry on this, for him, hopeless discovery, he is found turning his attention towards some means of supplying the rapidly increasing demand for spun cotton—cotton weft for the weaver's loom. He proceeds to put together the rudiments of his design, and although struggling with poverty, he resolves, in 1767 or 1768, being then settled down at Preston, his native town, to bring his spinning machine into use.

About the same time, a person named Hargreaves had obtained a patent for something of a similar purpose, and as Arkwright had already suffered much from the envy of others, he apprehended great obstruction in his design from Hargreaves, and consequently removed from his own neighbourhood to Nottingham, where he hoped to avoid that hindrance, and to get assistance in carrying out his designs. This, after some negotiation, he obtained from the highly respectable bankers, Messrs. Wright (a firm which still maintains its reputation), who advanced the means for carrying out his projects. They,

however, at length became tired, and introduced him to a
stocking-manufacturer of the name of Need, with whom he
entered into an arrangement. But Mr. Need also shortly
became weary; and being connected with Mr. Jedediah Strutt
of Derby, the principal founder of the great house at Belper,
and one of the ancestors of the late president of the Government Railway Board, that gentleman and Arkwright were
shortly afterwards brought together.

Mr. Strutt was himself a man of very considerable attainments in mechanics, and not long before had taken out a
patent for an improvement of the stocking-frame, which is
perhaps one of the most ingenious machines in existence, and
is now used in the formation of fabrics the dealing in which
constitutes one of our most extensive businesses. He pointed
out to Arkwright several deficiencies in his machine, which
all the inventive powers of the latter had been unable to
supply. These, however, with his suggestions, were soon
remedied; and, in 1769, Arkwright took out his first patent.
The principal peculiarity consisted in the application of two
pair of rollers, one pair thicker than the other, and placed at
a little distance from them. Both the under rollers were
fluted longitudinally like a crimping machine, and the upper
ones were covered with leather so that they were enabled to
take firm hold of the cotton as it passed through them.

The rollers were so managed that while the first pair
turned slowly the second were made to revolve with ten times
the rapidity, so that the cotton which came from between the
first hair in the form of a thick thread, was extended to ten
times the length and fineness after it had passed through the
second.

Mr. Strutt and Mr. Need became Arkwright's partners in
the concerns which it was intended to carry on under the
patent, and their first mill, which was turned by horse power,
was erected at Nottingham. The experiment was entirely

successful, and in 1771 they established another at Cromford in Derbyshire, in which water was the motive agent, and hence the yarn made by it acquired the name of *water twist* throughout the trade. By several combinations, which it is unnecessary to describe, Arkwright effected other improvements, for which a fresh patent was taken out in 1775.

For five years did these enterprising men work on without receiving a particle of profit; and it is a singular proof of the confidence of the two capitalists, Messrs. Strutt and Need, both in the abilities and the integrity of the inventor, that they were content to presevere for so long a period in the face of so much discouragement. The time for their reward, however, came at last. The tide of prosperity *did* at length flow, and it flowed abundantly—for wealth, perhaps, was never before so rapidly acquired in the ordinary course of business. Mr. Arkwright engaged in various other cotton manufactories beside the one in which he was most largely interested, and rose to the highest distinction in his particular sphere; was made high-sheriff of his county; and was, at last, knighted by King George III. But his sedentary life induced ill-health, and he at length sunk under a complication of disorders, on the 3rd of August, 1792, at the comparatively early age of sixty, respected by all who knew him, for his honourable character and his great business accomplishments. He left a fortune estimated at half a million of money, having for a number of years before his death, from time to time, regularly fixed the price of cotton yarn for all the trade.

The process of spinning cotton by machinery is so curious that it well deserves a description, however cursory, for it is a business of which everybody hears, but of which few have any correct idea.

The distaff gave way in England to the use of the spinning-wheel throughout the greater portion of the country in the reign of Henry VIII., but no further improvement was made in the process of turning the fibres of flax or cotton into thread till the middle of the last century, when the inventions of Arkwright for spinning, and of Hargreaves and Dr. Cartwright for weaving, opened the way for that immense extension of the business which has since taken place. The best system now pursued is as follows :—

The bags of cotton, when received from abroad, are far from being in a state fit for immediate use ; some seeds remain after the most careful cleaning ; and the pressure to which the cotton is subjected in packing, forms hard matted lumps, and some of the coarser and heavier wool is unavoidably mixed with that of superior quality. The first operation in the process of manufacture is consequently the cleaning of the cotton. It is put into the willowing machine, where it is torn open by revolving spikes, and subjected to the action of a very powerful blast, produced by the rapid turnings of a fan ; the light wool is thus blown to some distance from the heavier portions, the dirt, seeds, &c. This process is continued in the scutching machine, where the cotton is beaten by metallic blades making from 3000 to 5000 revolutions in the minute ; these completely open the fibre, and separate the fine wool from the waste, which falls to the ground through a frame of wire work. The wool is afterwards taken to the *spreading machine*, which is formed of rollers, and these, by compressing the wool, prepare it for the *carding* machine.

The original cards of the woollen woolcombers were nothing more or less than square pieces of board, with a number of pointed wires of equal length driven into their faces, and having handles at the back, by which workmen could tear and rend the locks of wool, so that their filaments might be brought parallel to each other. Hargreaves improved on this in 1760, by the substitution of a large *fixed card*, which was worked upon by others that were moveable, through the agency of a pulley fixed in the ceiling, so that several cards could be used at once.

But this modification was still further improved upon by another, which was first adopted by the grandfather of Sir R. Peel, at Blackburn, in 1762. The inventor of this is not precisely ascertained; but it has been ascribed to Paul, whom we have previously noticed as being connected with Mr. Wyatt, of Birmingham; for, in 1748, it is known that he took out a specification for carding, though it will be seen afterwards that it ought with more justice to be ascribed to Mr. Peel himself. Be it whose it may, it is an ingenious and highly useful instrument, consisting of a horizontal cylinder of about three feet in length, with a spiral card, or set of points projecting from its surface, which works under a fixed concave frame, with a set of similar points on its lower side. The cylinder is made to revolve at a very rapid rate, and as fast as the cotton is supplied, the points on the cylinder and the points on the frame act against each other, and the filaments of the cotton are all brought in a position parallel with each other. Fast as the wool reaches the extremity of the cylinder it is struck, rapidly and repeatedly, by a flat piece of metal, with short teeth at its upper edge, which detaches it from the cylinder, and it falls into an instrument which compresses it. It is then carried between other rollers, on its exit from which it appears in the form of a soft thick thread, and is then passed into the drawing frame, which is, in fact, Arkwright's original invention of a double set of rollers; through these it passes sometimes as many as a thousand times, until the whole substance is of one uniform thickness and texture.

The cotton is now one continuous cord, but in order to make it serviceable, a twist is necessary, and this is commonly given to it by a machine called a *fly frame*, for which a patent was taken out in 1817. It is provided with a number of spindles, which turn at a very rapid rate, and the revolutions give the requisite twist to the yarn, and deliver it at once to the bobbins, which are attached to the cylinders to receive it.

Ingenious, however, as this was, it was exceeded by a contrivance of Mr. Samuel Crompton's, who invented an instrument of a very complex character; the chief utility of which consists in its twisting and stretching the yarn at the same time to an uniform thinness. This is effected by a number of spindles which revolve at a somewhat more rapid rate than that portion of the machine from which the yarn is supplied, and are so managed as to recede from it to the length of fifty-four or fifty-six inches. As soon as the whole of these processes are performed, the mule disengages itself from those portions of the machine which have been used to propel it, and the attendant returns it again to the carriage to perform its work afresh.

MULE ROOM.

But the last great triumph of mechanical ingenuity in this branch of art was that for which a patent was taken out by Mr. Roberts, a machine-maker of Manchester, in 1830. It obviated the necessity of an attendant to take the spindle back to the carriage, for the mule not only disengaged itself, but, by an intervening contrivance, returned without any human aid to repeat its duty from the carriage, so that the only assistance required is merely that of a child to piece the threads when they happen to break : and such is the economy and the general advantages of this machine, that it has now come into very general use in the great manufactories, and it is universally adopted wherever new machinery has to be set up.

The yarn is now complete, and it has only to be prepared for sale for the home trade or for exportation. When it is to be used for weft in the factory where it is produced, it is at once applied to the shuttle, in the form in which it comes from the spindles, being then in a sort of conical shape, and known by the name of *cops;* but when it has to be used for warp, it is wound by means of a self-acting reel, impelled like all the other machinery by the steam-engine, into hanks of 840 yards long; each of these is tied round with a thread, and they are all then weighed to ascertain their fineness. When very fine yarns are required they are passed at an exceedingly rapid rate through coal gas flames, to take off their down and give them smoothness. These yarns are then pressed into bundles by means of a machine called a *bundle press,* which is of sufficient power to be worked by young women; and thus prepared they are ready to be transmitted once more across those wide seas which the material has already traversed, to supply the necessities of those distant lands where their feathery substance was first produced.

Cotton *thread* is made by laying two or more yarns side by side; these yarns are first passed through a thin solution of starch, and are then twisted together by means of machinery, in a way contrary to that in which they were wound by the spinning machine.

And now, what have been the advantages of this combination of intellect, industry, and capital? The quantity of cotton introduced into this country was only about 16,000,000 lbs.

when the inventions of Arkwright were under contemplation. It is now, however, close upon 400,000,000 lbs.; and the quantity of yarn, which at that time was nothing, is now upwards of 100,000,000 lbs.; and that which in the year 1786, after the business at Cromford was established, was sold for 38s. a pound, was, in 1800, reduced to 9s. 5d., and is now commonly disposed of at the rate of 1s. 7d. a pound.

Yet this invention, valuable as it is, would have been of comparatively little worth if there had not been some means of rendering it available for weaving by machinery. And by a singular accident this was accomplished. Some time during the year 1784, some gentlemen were in conversation upon the then recent invention of Arkwright's for spinning yarn, when one of them observed, that it would produce so much, that there would not be hands enough to weave it. The late Rev. Dr. Cartwright, brother to the celebrated Major Cartwright, who was one of the party, observed in reply, that Arkwright then must invent machinery for weaving also. This unpremeditated idea seems to have taken strong hold upon his mind, for he shortly afterwards set about the construction of a machine which should perform the three motions of weaving, and succeeded so far that in the following year he was enabled to take out a patent. This machine he endeavoured to bring into play by establishing a power-loom factory at Doncaster, but did not succeed. A similar misfortune attended the efforts of Messrs. Grimshawe at Manchester. Dr. Cartwright, however, still persevered, and contributed much to render the power loom what it is; but after taking out a number of patents, and spending upwards of £40,000, without any personal benefit, he relinquished the hope of fully accomplishing his object.

One of the chief impediments with which the inventors had to contend, was the frequent necessity for stopping the machine in order to dress the warp, which was continually liable to breakage; this was at length obviated by the ingenious invention of the *dressing machine* of Mr. Radcliffe, of Stockport, who was assisted by one of his workmen, named Johnson. This is a piece of mechanism consisting of eight rollers, four at one end of a frame and four at the other; these rollers are brought from the warping frame, and the yarns from these are made to pass between two rollers, the lower one of which dips into a reservoir of thin paste, and thus transfers a coating of starch to the cotton; the yarns afterwards pass over and under brushes, by which it is rubbed into the fibres, and then over a heated copper box to dry them, and are ultimately coiled round the warp beam of the loom. Some time after the invention of the dressing machine, two gentlemen, manufacturers at Stock-port, of the name of Marsland and Horrocks, fairly brought the steam engine into effective use, and Mr. Roberts, of the firm of Roberts and Sharp of Manchester, having introduced considerable improvements, the Power Loom became fully and effectively established.

In order that the weaving should be perfect, great care is necessary in all the preliminary arrangements of the warp yarn, which must be extended on the loom in parallel lines, and with an equal degree of tension. The rods which separate the alternate threads, technically called the lease-rods, are to be set so as to keep the threads which are to go through one heddle quite distinct from those belonging to the other. Having received his yarn in a bundle, the weaver first rolls it regularly on the yarn cylinder, keeping the threads distinct by an instrument called a ravel, which is in fact a coarse kind of reed. After the warp is wound on the cylinder, the operation of "drawing-in" commences; that is, the alternate threads are to be drawn through their respective healds or heddles, and all the threads through the dents of the reed. The instrument used in this process is called a sley, or reed-hook, and is so constructed as to take two threads through every dent or interval of the reed. The lease, or separation of the alternate threads in the warp yarn, is made by the pins in the warping mill, and is preserved by the lease rods. These rods being tied together at the ends, secure the permanency of the lease and guide the operative in drawing the alternate yarns through the heddles. To facilitate the process, the beam on which the warp yarn has been wound is suspended a little above the heddles, so as to allow the yarn to hang down

perpendicularly. The operative then opens the loop in each of the twines of the heddles successively, and through each draws a warp thread. This is, therefore, an operation not very unlike threading a needle, having its eye in the middle instead of the end. After the threads have been passed singly through the loops or eyes of the heddles, they are drawn in pairs through the dents of the reed. The heddles are then mounted with the cords by which they are moved, and the reed being placed in the batten, every thing is ready for the weaver to commence his operations.

The utility of the power loom was too evident to be overlooked by the shrewd and enterprising members of the British manufacturing community, and it consequently soon

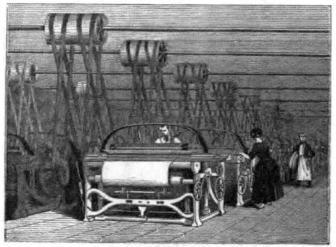

POWER LOOM ROOM.

came into general use. It was calculated by Mr. Baines some few years ago, that the number employed in England was upwards of 85,000, and 15,000 in Scotland, there being many factories with above a thousand in each, while there were above 300,000 hand looms, according to the last account, still in work.

But the cloth was still white, and though adapted for many useful purposes, it was still but little fit for the great object for which it has since been to such an immense extent adapted—attire.

Among others who began to be affected by the growing spirit of enterprise which, about the middle of the last century, pervaded the manufacturing interests throughout the North of England, was a farmer of little means who lived at the village of Blackburn in Lancashire. He was a man of observant and inquiring mind, shrewd, diligent, and energetic. Labour was of little consequence, provided an object was attained by it. He had remarked the tediousness of the process by which the raw cotton wool was brought into a state fit for spinning by the common hand card, and he it was, as there is almost every proof, that invented the cylinder for doing the work so much better and expeditiously. Success attended him here sufficiently to induce him altogether to give up farming; and seeing everybody busy about him, he adapted himself to another part of the business, and the farmer turned calico printer. He set to work, and with his own hands he cut away on blocks of wood with such tools as he could command till he had formed the figure of a parsley leaf. At the back of each of these blocks he put a handle, and put a little pin of strong wire at each of the four corners in front. Each of these blocks was ten inches long and five broad. He then got a tub, into which he put come coloured mixture with a little alum in it. He then covered the tub with a woollen cloth which sunk till it touched the colouring matter and became saturated with it. The calico was stretched tightly across the table top, and the quondam farmer of Blackburn then touched the woollen cloth with the face of his parsley leaf block, and soon as the figure was fairly covered with the colour he placed it squarely on the cloth and struck it sharply with a mallet, so that the figure of the engraving was left upon the white calico. The little points at the corners enabled him to repeat the process with regularity, and so he continued till the whole was complete. Soon as it was dry his wife and daughters set to work and ironed it with the common smoothing irons, and this they continued to do for some time. But the ingenious farmer was as little satisfied with the loss of time in this instance as he had previously been with the hand card, and having seen the good effect of a cylinder in that case, he determined to try it in this. He had an oblong frame made with a smooth wooden bottom and upright posts, and a rail on each side. Running from side to side there was a roller with a handle to turn it, and round the roller there was a rope wound round spirally. Each end of the rope was fastened to an oblong deep box, as wide and as long as the frame. It was filled with bricks, and of course was very heavy. The farmer had now a machine more forcible than the strength and warm irons of his wife and daughters. He therefore wound his pieces of calico round smooth wooden rollers which were placed under the box, and that being drawn backwards and forwards by means of the rope round the upper roller, the winch soon gave the requisite smoothness to the new work. This in truth was the *mangle* now used for domestic purposes, by which many a poor woman gains a livelihood.

It was afterwards superseded by superior machinery worked on more complex but not more scientific principles. But it answered the purpose admirably. The farmer worked on; his goods were readily bought, and he was much sought after, for the cautious fellow kept his knowledge to himself. And so he went on, step by step, till he became the head of one of the largest houses in the country. His eldest son joined him in business, and the tide of affluence flowed fast and constantly upon the firm. With the wealth thus acquired, at a time of great national emergency, the son raised at his own expense a regiment of horse for the general defence, and the Government made him a baronet. His son, whose name, like his own and his father's, was Robert, he brought up well and sent to college, where the young man, by good abilities and diligence, obtained great distinction. He afterwards obtained a seat in parliament, lived to sway senates by his word, and ultimately became the prime minister of an empire whose power never was excelled, and the extent of which never was equalled.

The name of the humble farmer of Blackburn, the self-taught calico printer, the inventor of the mangle, the founder of a family which in two generations has risen to an equality with the oldest nobility in the land—that farmer's name was Peel.

Mr. Peel was however not content with hard labour, even facilitated as it was by his own inventions, and he accordingly removed to a place called Brookside, about two miles from Blackburn, for the sake of water, and there, by the assistance of his sons, extended his business very considerably.

In 1773 his eldest son, Robert, who had always been his chief support, left the concern and entered into partnership with a Mr. Yates, and his uncle, whose name was Haworth, and with them carried on an extensive business at the town of Bury. Two other sons entered into partnership and established their business at a place called Church, and were, like their elder brother and their father, eminently successful.

The principle of block printing, however, was found too slow, especially when more than one colour was to be used, and cylinders were again adopted. The pattern to be printed was engraved on the face of a cylinder (and to the credit of this adoption, Mr. Peel appears to be peculiarly entitled), which revolves in connexion with another of equal size. The lower cylinder, on which the pattern was wrought, turns with half its circumference in a box which contains colouring matter, which in the course of its progress is shaved off by a blade of soft steel, except where the pattern is engraved. The cloth is passed between the two cylinders and receives the impression of the pattern; it is afterwards passed over another cylinder filled with hot steam, and almost instantly dried. Where three or four colours are to be used, there must be as many cylinders, and thus a piece of calico, of twenty-eight yards in

63

length, can be printed, in various colours, in about two minutes—
a work which, by hand labour, could not be performed in less
than a week.

But another improvement was made. These cylinders had
been usually made of copper, and they were not only expensive
to engrave, but soon wore out; and it was therefore an immense advantage to the calico printers when a plan was adopted
for reducing that expense. This system was, to engrave a very
small steel cylinder, of two or three inches in length, with the
pattern desired, when the metal was in what is called the decar-
bonised, or softened state, after which it was attempered till it
became very hard. When it was hardened to the utmost, it
was worked by powerful machinery against a large cylinder,
which, being duly softened, received the design; that also was
in its turn hardened, and then worked against the copper
roller, which received the impression as originally engraved,
and thus was fitted for the printing process.

At this point it was that chemistry—that strange and
wonderful science, which more, perhaps, than any other, has
unlocked the secrets of nature—came in to the assistance of
art. A substance was discovered, called *chlorine*, which has
the peculiar property of discharging all vegetable colours, and
thus, with a magic exceeding all the tales of romance, bleached
the cloth to a fairer and purer white in a few hours, than could
by the old process of exposure to the air, on the grass, have
been obtained in many months. And this was of inestimable
value, for in order to print the richest patterns, the most
perfect white that could be obtained was necessary.

But a complaint was made that, however beautiful, the
prints would not *wash*, and consequently, when once dirtied, a
dress became useless, and the earth was ransacked to obtain
what are called *mordants*, for the several colours. The term,
it is almost needless to say, is derived from the French word
mordre, to bite, as it seems to make the colour bite into the

cloth and become fixed, and one of the plans adopted was to
print the cloth with the mordant only, then to dip it in the
dying vat, and afterwards wash it out, when the mordant was
found to have retained the pattern in beautiful integrity.
Another plan is to print the pattern with lemon juice; the
piece is then steeped in the mordant, dried quickly, and dyed
in the vat. When washed, the acid is found to have resisted
the mordant, and the pattern stands out in pure white, all the
rest of the cloth of course retaining the colour in which it was
dyed. This is called *discharge work*, and gave to the Peels an
opportunity of imitating very beautifully the Indian patterns
which were at that time very much admired, and obtained for
their house a character which never was lost, for it enabled
them to produce goods, excellent in every respect, both for
beauty and fastness of colour.

There was, however, another discovery made by a person
named Grouse, a commercial traveller of London, who, although
utterly destitute of anything like scientific knowledge, is stated
to have been fond of fireside experiments. He sold his invention to
the late Sir R. Peel, the father of the present statesman, for
five pounds, and there is little doubt but that the person who
bought it realized more than fifty thousand times that sum by
it. The process is called *resist work*, and it consists in printing
the cloth with a kind of paste and then dying it with indigo;
and after being properly dried, it is found that the paste has
resisted the colouring matter, and the pattern is left of a pure
and beautiful white colour. Without the paste the indigo
would not wash out, and this is the means through which these
beautiful blue dresses with the white spots, which no one can
see without admiring, are made.

All this, however, was not sufficient. It was not enough to
have utility, durability, and neatness, for beauty of design was
also requisite to satisfy the ripening faculties and the improve-
ing character which a long period of peace has brought out,

and all the efforts of the most ingenious artists have been put into requisition to attain that object. That it has at length been attained is evident to all, but it is a singular coincidence that the person by whom it has been chiefly accomplished is also a farmer's son, who, by his honourable conduct, and by the persevering exercise of his excellent abilities, attained to wealth and position, and who was in his turn enabled in seven short years to break down opinions and unsettle notions centuries old, and is at the present moment receiving the homage of every country in Europe for his moral courage and pre-eminent ability. The individual of whom we are speaking is Richard Cobden.

THE BIRTH-PLACE OF THE FIRST SIR ROBERT PEEL AT BLACKBURN.

THE ARRIVAL OF THE GREAT WESTERN STEAM-SHIP AT NEW YORK.

STEAM-NAVIGATION.

MOST boys have either heard or read of the astonishment of the South Sea Islanders on first beholding
a ship in full sail, which they mistook for some
monstrous aquatic bird, floating along with its wings
uplifted, like the swan, to catch the breeze.   The astonishment evinced by the rustic populace of England was almost
like that of the savages when first steam-boats appeared in
our rivers; and we can remember the time when the wondering villagers walked many a weary mile to see a vessel going
against wind and tide, without either oar or sail to propel it
along.   Grey-headed old men and women, who had dwelt
beside the river for more than half a century, and had seen the

vessels tack about from shore to shore, as they made a little headway by shifting the sails and catching the wind, stood with uplifted hands, and staring eyes, and mouths agape, when they saw the little steamer dashing against the current, and with the wind right a-head, passing field and farm and hamlet, as if pushed along by some hidden and gigantic hand. They saw the chimney arise like the neck of the extinct plesisauris, that heaved up above the mastless seas of the early world, showing at times its dusk body, but never revealing the immense fins or paddles by which it oared itself along; and as they gazed, they were almost disposed to believe that this monster of the fossil world had come again to

"Fright the isle from its propriety."

They had been from childhood familiar with shipping; but, excepting when a strong and favourable wind blew, had only been accustomed to see the vessels move according to the ebb and flow of the river—now making slow progress for about twelve hours, then laying by until the tide turned, and the current was again in their favour; and when the rains descended from the hilly countries, and the tide had no power to turn the headlong waters, for days not a ship came from the direction of the sea, until the steamer flapped its paddles, and came up the river snorting like a sea-horse, and bidding defiance to wind, flood, and tide, as it rolled triumphant over the roaring current. No marvel that in those days the banks of the rivers were lined with wondering faces, and that old men and women asked each other what the world would be fifty years hence.

Nor did their astonishment end here—for the steam-tug next appeared, dragging the large and heavily-laden merchant's ship behind it, as if to say, " Come along, you great lubber, and don't lay sulking there at the mouth of the river, when the grocers want tea, and sugar, and coffee. Keep fast hold of my hand, and I 'll pull you through, although I am but a little fellow, and the current is so strong, and the wind blows in my face, and I am half-blinded by the spray; yet I 've got such a spirit within me, that I shall never give up until I 've brought you safe to the wharf beside the town, where everybody will be glad and ready to receive you." And but for the steam-boat, wagons would have had to have gone for miles and miles round over-land; and the dangerous ferry-boat would have been employed to cross the rapid and high-swollen river, and perhaps have been carried away for miles by the rushing waters, and—as we remember in more than one instance—out into the open sea. Then the slow motion of those old-fashioned brigs, sloops, keels, market-boats, catches, barges, and cuckoos, which were sometimes hauled along by horses, but oftener by men ·and boys, with ropes around their shoulders, moving at such a snail-like pace— never more than two miles an hour. You could count every pane in a cottage window while they passed; but in the steam-boat, weed and willow, and style and grange, seemed to dance by you, and all the landscape to move. Such were the changes made in inland navigation by the introduction of steamers; while on the ocean, greater marvels were wrought.

One of the greatest aids rendered to civilization by the discovery of the steam-engine was the increase it gave to the speed of human locomotion. We must bear in mind, that whoever multiplies and renders easier the means of intercourse between the different races of mankind, is a reformer in the purest sense of the word; for the cause of human progress is advanced by our seeing and learning more of each other, and by the mutual interchange of opinions and ideas. Without well-constructed roads, this beneficial intercourse cannot take place even between citizens of the same island-country; and while navigation continued dependent on winds and tides, all intercourse with other countries, and especially distant ones, was of course still more restricted. Before steam lent its giant powers to the propulsion of ships, locomotion over the waters of the deep was attended with so much danger and uncertainty that, as a common proverb, it became the type and the representative of everything which was precarious and perilous. The application, however, of steam to navigation has rescued the mariner and the voyager from many of the dangers of wind and water; and even in its present state, putting out of view its probable improvement, it has rendered all voyages of moderate length very nearly as safe and regular as journeys over-land.

The method of moving vessels by paddle-wheels was often adopted by the Romans, and even by the ancient Egyptians; but the wheels were merely turned by handles within the vessels. De Garay's experiment, already noticed in our account of the steam-engine, is supposed to have consisted of the propulsion of paddle-wheels by steam; and long after his time boats were moved by paddle-wheels, though not by the agency of steam, however, in various countries of Europe. In England, for instance, Prince Rupert is related to have challenged King Charles I. to compete with him in a boat-race upon the Thames; and it is further stated that, by using paddle-wheels, the prince succeeded in getting his boat along at a rate equal to twelve miles an hour. There is also, in the Marquis of Worcester's "Century of Inventions," written in 1655, though not published for eight years later, an obscure statement in reference to a vessel being moved by steam, "which should, if need be, pass London Bridge against the current at low water."

Eighteen or twenty years after the publication of the Marquis of Worcester's book, Captain Savary made some attempts to use a steam, or rather an atmospheric engine, to urge a vessel along, but could not carry out his design to any useful effect. About the same time, too, Denis Papin, an ingenious French philosopher, was endeavouring to prove theoretically how this object might be effected; and he went so far as to lay his plan in detail before the Royal Society, with an offer to put it in practice for the small advance of fifteen pounds towards the expenses. This offer, however, was rejected; chiefly, it is believed, from the Society being at that time in very straightened circumstances. Half a century later, Jonathan Hulls took out a patent for moving vessels by steam power, which vessels were to be used for the purpose of towing other vessels, as the inventor considered it preferable to have the machinery in a separate vessel by itself. The scheme, however, was never put into practice; and other inventions, which met with no better success, followed at intervals. Among the rest, one by M. Genevois, a pastor of Berne, which consisted of a species of steam-propeller, formed like the foot of a duck, to expand and present a large surface to the water when moved against it, and to close up into a small compass when moved in an opposite direction. At length, in 1774, the Comte D'Auxiron, a French nobleman, succeeded in the construction of a boat, which, when tried upon the Seine near Paris, moved against the stream, though slowly, the engine being of insufficient power. In his efforts he was assisted by an ingenious countryman of his, named Perier, who, in the year following the termination of his connexion with the Comte, placed a boat upon the river, with an engine of one horse power, and one paddle; but his means were also insufficient for the purpose, and the boat was ultimately broken up. Perier ascribed his failure to the form of the paddle, which he conceived to be an inefficient substitute for oars, and he adopted several plans to obviate what he conceived to be the difficulty. But there was no useful result; and his endeavours excited little notice even in his own country.

Three years after the failure of these experiments,

according to a statement of M. Arago, in an historic sketch of the progress of steam, published in 1837, the Marquis de Jouffroy made attempts on a large scale at Beaume-les-Danes, and again tried a boat of considerable size on the Saone, at Lyons. This endeavour excited much attention, and all the authorities agree in the assertion that the vessel used was upwards of 120 feet long and not less than 15 feet beam. The dreadful disturbances which shortly afterwards broke out in France put a stop to his efforts; and for several years he was an exile from his native country. On his return, in 1796, he found the principal part of his invention adopted by a person named Des Blancs, a watchmaker at Trevoux, who had assiduously gathered information respecting the proceedings of the marquis. The latter appealed to the government; but Des Blancs had obtained a patent during his absence, so that he was left without any redress. Robert Fulton, who afterwards occupied an important position in reference to steam-navigation, was at that time experimenting in France, and had adopted a series of float-boards, which were moved by an endless chain stretched over two wheels that projected on either side of the boat; but he ultimately abandoned the plan and used paddles. Des Blancs complained of the infringement of his patent; and Fulton, after showing him the difference bebetween the two machines, offered a portion of the advantages if he would bear a portion of the expense of the trials; but no arrangement appears to have been entered into between them. Neither Des Blancs nor his country obtained any advantage from his efforts; and this appears to have been nearly all that was done in France for steam navigation before the close of the last century.

The enterprising spirit of the Americans was not likely to suffer them to be wanting in efforts to bring that to pass which had caused so much sensation on this side of the Atlantic, and which, even at that time, promised such immense results.

Accordingly, we find that two individuals, named Rumsey and Fitch, were engaged in active rivalry in the United States in applying the steam-engine to the impulsion of vessels. The latter of these two gentlemen, as early as 1783, was occupied in the construction of a boat, which he afterwards contrived to move with paddles, by the aid of a steam-engine, on the Delaware; and in 1785, he had so far completed his design that he presented a model of his apparatus to Congress. He was encouraged by the support of several wealthy men who provided the means for his experiments, and was so sanguine of success as to express his firm conviction that the ocean would ultimately be crossed by steam-vessels—a declaration which, when it was made, must have appeared to be little else than the notion of a visionary, but which many of his generation have lived to see so wonderfully realized.

Rumsey, his rival, was also backed by a company; and in 1784 succeeded in the construction of a boat, a model of which in that year he exhibited to General Washington. This vessel was about fifty feet long, and was carried along the Potomac by means of a stream of water which, with a pump worked by a steam-engine, entered at the bow and was carried out at the stern, the reaction of the water being the impelling agent. The boiler only held about five gallons, and the fuel consumed was about six bushels of coal in twelve hours. Yet with this imperfect apparatus—when the boat was loaded with three tons weight, beside the engine, which was about a third of a ton more—he succeeded in attaining a rate of three or four miles an hour. Rumsey afterwards came to England, and by the assistance of some capitalists he built another vessel, which was tried on the Thames, in the month of February, 1793; and in several trials made afterwards, one attained a speed, against wind and tide, of upwards of four miles an hour.

About the same year, Mr. Lineaker, the master shipwright of Portsmouth dockyard, began a series of experiments on the same principle; and at length so far succeeded as to be induced, in the year 1808, to take out a patent for securing the benefit of his invention.

Although these several experiments, on which so much ingenuity, money, and labour had been expended, were insufficient for the establishment of steam-navigation, they were nevertheless useful in promoting that important object by making its principles better understood. The very failures were in themselves beneficial, inasmuch as they showed what had to be avoided, as well as what was required; and, by the happy union of experience, skill, suggestive faculty, and wealth, this was at length fully accomplished.

A country gentleman of Dalswinton, named Patrick Miller, one of that class who find pleasure in devoting both their property and their time to the furtherance of objects of public utility, having long been a patient observer of the efforts made to construct steam-vessels, and having a fine lake in the park of Dalswinton House, in Dumfriesshire, at length began to experiment. He had for some years been engaged in the improvement of naval architecture, and had proposed to build ships of much greater length, in proportion to their breadth, than any that had been previously used; but he found them unable to bear the sail which was requisite to drive them through the water. To obviate this defect he proposed to use paddle-wheels, to be moved by some power within the vessel, as auxiliary to the wind; and for that purpose he had a boat built with a double keel, so as to obtain what he conceived to be a proper position for working them.

In 1785, Mr. James Taylor went to reside with Mr. Miller, as a tutor to his younger sons, and during the two following years repeatedly assisted him in his experiments on Dalswinton Lake. In 1787, one of these double-bottomed boats, sixty feet long, propelled by paddles moved by two men, was matched against a fast-sailing vessel belonging to the Custom House authorities; and both Miller and Taylor perceived the insufficiency of the power to turn the wheels. To remedy this defect, the latter suggested the use of the steam-engine; but Mr. Miller was dubious of its utility, and besides, knew not where to find the individual who could render it applicable. At that time, it should be recollected it was simply, or almost entirely, used as a pumping-machine. Again Mr. Taylor was of service, and, through his agency, William Symington was introduced to the proprietor of Dalswinton. Symington, with whom Taylor was in correspondence, had been for some years engaged in the attempt to acquire a rotatory motion from the steam-engine, and in the construction of a steam-carriage. The model of this he showed to Mr. Miller, whom he met for the first time, toward the latter end of 1787, at the house of his patron, Mr. Gilbert Meason, in Edinburgh. The result of that interview was a determination to construct an engine of about one horse power, which was placed in a small double-bottomed pleasure-boat in the course of the following year. This boat had the engine on one side, the boiler on the other, and the paddle in the middle; and with all the hindrances of a first experiment, they attained a speed of five miles an hour.

This was accomplished in a manner to induce further trial, and, in the next year, Mr. Miller had a twelve horse engine cast, and it was fixed in the same double bottomed boat just spoken of. Some difficulty was experienced in consequence of the breaking of the float-boards, from the great strain of the engine; but the trial, which was shortly afterwards made on the Clyde and Forth canal, was perfectly successful; a speed of seven or eight miles an hour was attained—a rate as great as that which, even in the present day, is generally reached in canal navigation. Thus was this great step achieved. Steam-navigation was now accomplished; and it only remained to show its immediate commercial utility. Mr. Miller, after having expended a handsome fortune in obtaining this great public benefit, retired from its further pursuit, and left others to work out its great results. Symington, however, still continued to persevere; and in 1801 commenced a series of successful experiments under the patronage of Lord Dundas. His object was to employ steam-vessels as tug-boats; and with one, which was built by him, he was enabled to draw, in 1802, two vessels loaded with seventy tons of goods at a considerable rate on the Clyde and Forth Canal, in a day when the wind was so strong a-head that no other vessel could move in the same direction.

Evident as was the success thus attained, the invention remained in comparative neglect for a considerable time. Symington had not the means, nor perhaps the qualities, of commercial energy and enterprise, necessary to stem the tide of public opinion, and to bring about so great a change, as that of substituting a novel moving power, for the ordinary means of navigation.

Many attempts have been made and much representation used to obtain for Fulton, who was originally an American artist, the credit of first using steam locomotion on the water; but although he possessed much inventive genius, and had been engaged with Chancellor Livingston, who was at the time minister for the United States at Paris, in the construction of vessels to be propelled by steam, still he never accomplished anything until after he had seen the vessels of Symington,

ROBERT FULTON.

and had been on a successful voyage with him in Scotland, when, according to Symington's account, Fulton made notes of everything that was shown him. Fulton appears to have been let into all Symington's secrets. Everything connected with the experiments of the latter for the accomplishment of steam-navigation was shown to Fulton, and all he did not comprehend was explained to him. It is true that in the plea for a patent, jointly sued for by Fulton and Livingston, the former claimed the right as an inventor; but there is no apparent ground for such an assumption, and the honour is sufficient for him to have been the first to have brought it into great practical application. Chancellor Livingston having supplied the means, a vessel was launched upon the Hudson, by Fulton, early in the spring of 1807. By the assistance of engineers from the works of Messrs. Bolton and Watt at Birmingham, the engines were completed in August, and everything was ready for the trip by the commencement of the new year; and the first attempt to navigate the waters of the New World by the aid of steam was made in January 1808. Fulton thus described to a friend the disheartening circumstances under which the construction of the first steam-boat—nicknamed by the Americans "Fulton's Folly"—was patiently persevered with by himself. He observes: "When I was building my first steam-boat at New York, the project was viewed by the public either with indifference, or with contempt, as a visionary scheme. My friends, indeed, were civil, but they were shy. They listened with patience to my explanations, but with a settled cast of incredulity on their countenances. As I had occasion to pass daily to and from the building-yard while my boat was in progress, I have often loitered unknown near the idle groups of strangers, gathering in little circles, and heard various inquiries as to the object of this new vehicle. The language was uniformly that of scorn, or sneer, or ridicule. The loud laugh often rose at my expense; the dry jest; the wise calculations of losses and expenditures; the dull but endless repetition of the Fulton Folly. Never did a single encouraging remark, a bright hope, a warm wish, cross my path. Silence itself was but politeness, veiling its doubts, or hiding its reproaches."

It is not surprising that by those who were called practical men the idea was considered as impracticable, illusory, and ridiculous; but when the trial really came, in the words of Fulton's biographer, " the minds of the most incredulous were changed in a few minutes. Before the boat had made the progress of a quarter of a mile the greatest unbeliever was converted! The man, who while he had looked on the expensive machine, thanked his stars that he had more sense than to waste his money on such idle schemes, changed the expression of his features as the boat moved from the wharf and gained her speed: the jeers of the ignorant, who had neither sense nor feeling enough to repress their contemptuous ridicule, were silenced for the moment by a vulgar astonishment which deprived them of the power of utterance, till the triumph extorted, from the incredulous multitude which crowded the shores, shouts and acclamations of congratulation and applause!"

The vessel was called the Clermont, from the name of Mr. Livingston's country residence; and she made her first voyage from New York to Albany, a distance of about a hundred and forty miles, at the average rate of five miles an hour; stopping some time at Clermont to take in water and coals. The whole of the progress up the Hudson was a continued triumph. Those on board of the several vessels which she met, looked with astonishment at the progress of a ship, which appeared to be a thing instinct with life rather than a fabric moved by mechanical means. It was said that to them " she had the most terrific appearance. The first steamers, as many in America yet do, used dry pine-wood for fuel, which sent forth a column of ignited vapour many feet above the flue, and whenever the fire was stirred, a galaxy of sparks flew off, and in the night had a very beautiful appearance. Notwithstanding the wind and tide were adverse to its approach, they saw with astonishment that the vessel was rapidly coming towards them; and when it came so near that the noise of the machinery and paddles were heard, the crews, in some instances, shrunk beneath their decks from the terrific sight, and left their vessels to go ashore, while others prostrated themselves and besought Providence to protect them from the approach of the horrible monster, which was marching on the tide, and lighting its path by the fire which it vomited."

Although success was complete, the Clermont, which was of a hundred and sixty tons burthen, did not make so great a speed as her projector anticipated, owing, in all probability, to an imperfection in the proportion of the paddle-wheels, which were fifteen feet in diameter, and dipped two feet in the water, impelled by a machine of four feet stroke and a two foot cylinder. She, however, continued to run during the season, occasionally requiring repairs, and at last was laid up for the winter, to be brought out in the following year with increased efficiency.

But the Clermont was not left to take all the honours, for there soon appeared a competitor in this new field of enterprise. Within a few weeks Mr. Stevens of Hoboken launched a steam-vessel, which, as she could not ply on the waters of the Hudson in consequence of the exclusive patent of Messrs. Fulton and Livingston, he took round to the Delaware; and this was the first steamer that ever braved the tides of the ocean. His son, Mr. R. L. Stevens, greatly improved upon the model of Fulton, and gave to the vessels which he built that elegant and commodious run by which many of them are now distinguished; acquiring not only beauty of form but the greater capability of cutting with speed through the water, so that some of his boats attained as great a rate as thirteen miles an hour. From that time steam-boats multiplied till every water in the civilized portions of America were studded with these rapid agents of intercourse, as various in their size and power as in the uses for which they were designed.

It was not till nearly four years after this that steam-navigation became practically useful, in the common sense of the term, in the British Isles; but there seems to be something like a coinciding propriety in the fact that it was also a Scotchman by whom it was first made available for the purposes of commerce and social intercourse on this side of the Atlantic.

Among the persons who had been acquainted with the experiments of Mr. Miller and his associates on the riyer Forth, was Mr. Henry Bell of Glasgow, an individual who had been the medium of communication between Fulton and the Scotch coadjutors, and who had sent to the former drawings of the boat and engines which they had used. Some time after Fulton had received these drawings, he wrote to Bell to say that he had constructed a boat from them, which prompted his correspondent to turn his attention to the introduction of steam-navigation in his own country. He accordingly set to work, but had to make several models before he was satisfied. At length he put one into the hands of Messrs. John Wood and Co., of Port Glasgow, who, from it, built for him a vessel of forty feet keel and ten feet six inches beam. This he fitted with an engine and paddles, and gave her the name of Comet, from the circumstance of the appearance of one of those celestial bodies in Scotland towards the latter end of the year in which she was launched. This vessel he was enabled to turn to profitable account; for, being a builder, he had erected a bath-house and hotel at Helensburgh, a watering-place on the opposite side of the Clyde, and he employed the Comet to transport passengers across the river, and thus derived a double advantage from it. The vessel was of about forty tons burthen, with an engine of three horse power: the engine being placed on one side and the boiler on the other, while the funnel was bent round, so as to rise in the middle of the deck, and serve the purpose, or seem to serve the purpose, of a mast. This vessel began to run in January 1812, and continued to ply throughout the following summer. She was moved at first by mere paddles, and attained a speed of five miles an hour; but her owner subsequently substituted wheels, having four paddles to each, of a malt-shovel form.

Soon after this success was fully proved, Mr. Hutchinson, a brewer at Glasgow, determining to share in the profits of steam navigation, had a vessel begun in March under the direction of Mr. Thomson, an engineer who had been engaged in some of the experiments made by Bell. She was finished in the following year, and was the second vessel that ever plied on the Clyde. She was larger than the Comet, being fifty-eight feet long, twelve feet beam, and five feet deep; she had engines of ten horse power. She was called the Elizabeth, and performed the distance between Greenock and Glasgow, twenty-seven miles, twice a-day. She must have been a fast boat, for it is stated by her owner that she often completed her voyage, with a hundred passengers aboard, in less than three hours.

About the time that Mr. Bell was preparing his steam-vessel, by a singular coincidence, a person named Dawson was, in Ireland, occupied on the very same project. The boat built by him was about fifty tons burthen, and was fitted with a high pressure engine; and by another similar coincidence, she was also called the Comet.

The success of these enterprises was not likely to pass unnoticed by the ship-owners and builders in the greatest port in the world; and we find, in the year 1814, a small packet, which had been built during the previous year, appointed to ply between London and Richmond. Another vessel, built by a gentleman at Bristol, was sent to London, through the canals, and assigned for the Gravesend station; but such was the opposition of the watermen, that she was withdrawn. But another, called the Margory, about seventy tons, which had been built by Messrs. Wood, on the Clyde, was brought round from Leith, and made her first trip from London to Gravesend on the 23rd of January, 1815. She continued to run between the two places during the following summer, but was frequently laid up for repairs. Shortly after, she was followed by another, about seventy-five tons burthen, with engines of sixteen horse power, and wheels of nine feet diameter. This vessel was also built by Messrs. Wood, on the Clyde, and was the first that ever performed any extensive sea-voyage. When launched, she was called the Glasgow; but that name was afterwards altered for the Thames, and she was brought round from Scotland, by her owner, Mr. Dodd, by means of both sail and steam, having to contend with some very rough weather in the Irish Sea. The narrative given by one of the passengers of that portion of the voyage between Dublin and London is so very interesting, that we shall transcribe a few paragraphs from it. When the vessel arrived at Dublin, the passenger in question, Mr. Weld, obtained permission from the captain, Mr. Dodd— formerly an officer in the Navy, and an engineer of great ability, having been the projector of Waterloo Bridge, and of the Thames Tunnel, which he proposed to carry across from Gravesend to Tilbury — to accompany him throughout the remainder of the voyage; and on Sunday, the 28th of May, 1815, they steamed out of the Liffey at noon, in the presence of many thousand spectators. Mr. Weld says, " We soon left far behind us all the vessels which sailed from Dublin with the same tide as we had done; and the following morning about nine o'clock we were off Wexford. The dense smoke which issued from our mast-chimney was observed from the heights above that town, and it was concluded that our vessel was on fire. All the pilots immediately put to sea to assist us; and on the arrival of the first boat alongside, it is impos-. sible to describe the excessive surprise, mingled with disappointment, when they saw that we were in no danger whatever, and that their hopes of salvage were at an end."

The weather becoming very stormy, the captain put into the port of Wexford for a few hours, when the vessel again proceeded on its voyage, and was again delayed for a short time to give rest to the engineer. On reaching the Isle of Ramsay, off the Irish coast, at this place several boats went to the vessel's assistance, on the same supposition that deceived the Wexford pilots, namely, that the ship was on fire. On putting out to sea again, "the weather had become unfavourable, and the sea ran alarmingly high in the bay. The waves, indeed, were of such magnitude, that when engulfed between them, the coast, although very lofty, could not be seen; but the vessel held her way most gallantly over all. A small fleet of merchant vessels left the straits of Ramsay with us, but in the passage of the bay alone we had left them so far behind as to be able to see only their masts." After passing the dangerous passage called Jack's Sound, and those fatal rocks known as " the Bishop and his Clerks," the vessel steered into the harbour of Milford Haven, meeting, on its way, the mail-packet proceeding from thence to Waterford with all her sails spread. After having passed it about a quarter of a mile, the Thames was put about, and sailed twice round the packet-ship while it was proceeding on its course, when some letters, written by the steamboat passengers, were put on board. At Milford the steamer excited a great amount of curiosity, more especially among the naval profession; and after meeting with other adventures, it set out to brave the dangers of the passage round the Land's End. Mr. Weld thus describes this portion of the voyage: " In doubling Cornwall Head, the most northern of those two great promontories which terminate England on the west, a tremendous swell met us coming from the Atlantic, whilst the tide, which ran strongly down St. George's Channel, combining with the swell, raised the waves to such a height as to render our position most alarming. The vessel appeared to suffer considerably, and the repeated concussions against the paddle-boxes terrified the pilot, who heard them for the first time. Night approached without any port being within reach excepting that which we had left, and which was now too distant to think of returning to. Such was the state of things when Captain Dodd observed that the vessel sailed better before the waves than in any other direction; he therefore spread some sails, and made a long tack, close-hauled, so as to get out of the latitude when the swell struggled against the tide, and at the end of some hours we doubled the Land's End, and found ourselves in a comparatively tranquil sea."

When the Thames reached Portsmouth, the utmost excitement prevailed on the part of the spectators in the harbour; and so many vessels came alongside, that the captain of the steamer was forced to request from the admiral to allow him a guard, that by this means some degree of order might be preserved. Some idea may be formed of the excitement, when it is stated that some officers, sitting at the time in court-martial, hurried off immediately, that they might obtain a sight of the surprising novelty. From Portsmouth the steamer proceeded to Margate, where, after stopping a day, it started off for London, passing every fast-sailing vessel it met with during the passage.

A year later, a vessel called the Majestic, which had been used as a towing-boat, and had once been as far as Calais, was employed to run between London and Margate; and two vessels, called respectively the London and the Richmond, were used, about the same time, to ply between the two places whose names they bore; and as they had to pass under bridges, they were provided with an apparatus of Dodd's, contrived for lowering the chimney. Another vessel, called the Sons of Commerce, ran between London and Margate; and, once performed the distance of eighty-eight miles in something more than seven hours and a half. There was also another vessel, called the Caledonia, on the same station, which had once crossed over to Flushing.

In 1818, so much had the principle of steam-navigation spread, that besides the vessels, then numerous, on the Thames, there were two on the Trent, four on the Humber, two on the Tyne, one on the Orwell, eighteen on the Clyde, two on the Tay, two at Dundee, six on the Forth, two at Cork, two on the Mersey, three on the Yare, one on the Avon, one on the Severn, and two intended to run between Dublin and Holyhead. Besides these, there were others in active employment in Russia, France, Spain, and the Netherlands; and a large number on the great rivers of the United States.

The great increase in the amount of horse-power that had at this time taken place in the engines of steam-vessels over that originally thought to have been sufficient when the Comet was built, necessarily resulted in the engines occupying considerably more space. To obviate this objection, high-pressure engines were employed; but, in spite of the precautions of the owners of the vessels, accidents frequently took place. In some inquiry which took place before a committee of the House of Commons in reference to this matter, Mr. Maudslay, the eminent engineer, thus expresses his opinion on the subject :—" As far as my opinion goes," he observes, " I would not go from here to Margate in a high-pressure boat, because there are many reasons why that may become much more dangerous, and no more advantageous to the public generally, or to the individuals. A low-pressure engine has a very high power; a high-pressure engine has a higher power, according to its height of steam. It is pretty well understood that a gentleman who engages in a Steamboat Company seldom attends to the engine himself, but leaves it to his men. I built the Regent steamboat last summer, with a low-pressure engine. There was a dispute between two men, and one of them swore that he would blow his boiler up but he would beat the Regent in coming up. The man certainly did exert himself as much as he could, and kept his steam as high as he could get it, and it flew out of the safety-valve very frequently; and he hurt his boiler very materially by doing so, but he did not beat the Regent; but if it had been a high-pressure engine, he would either have beat her or blown up his boiler, because he had the power in his own hands."

Up to this period, although there had been isolated voyages by sea to get from one station to another, there had been no regular passages made. The delay which was often experienced by the sailing packets in traversing the stormy channel between Holyhead and Dublin, suggested the adoption of steam to obviate it; and Dodd and his friends made repeated proffers to Government to provide the vessels for that purpose, if they were preferred for the contract, for carrying the Irish mails. But their offers were declined, and again it was destined that a Scotchman should be the leader in an enterprise to open up this great social improvement. The first vessel that ever sped regularly across the sea was the Rob Roy, a ship of about ninety tons burthen, and thirty horse power, the property of Mr. David Napier, one of a family at Glasgow, almost every member of which became distinguished for eminence in mechanical science. This vessel he appointed to run between Greenock and Belfast, a voyage which she performed during the stormy months of winter, although steamers had only been out previously during the summer season; and after running for two years there, she was transferred to the station of Calais and Dover, as a government packet.

But the enterprising spirit of Mr. Napier was not to be satisfied with such success as this. In 1819, he employed Messrs. Wood to build a vessel of a hundred and fifty tons burthen, with two engines of thirty horse power each, which he called the Talbot, followed by another called the Ivanhoe—both the finest and most complete vessels of the time. These ships were placed on the Holyhead Station, to run between that port and Dublin, and assist the sailing packets, which carried the mails; but such was their speed and regularity that they very quickly superseded them. Other vessels were added afterwards, which were strengthened by diagonal framing under the direction of Sir Robert Seppings, the Surveyor of the Navy. According to the evidence given before the Select Committee for investigating the condition of the Holyhead Roads, and for ascertaining what facilities could be given for expediting the communication between England and Ireland, it appeared that while one hundred mails by the sailing packets had, owing to the wind and other accidents of a sea voyage, been behind their proper time of arriving at the post office, only twenty-two, even in the most stormy state of the Irish Sea, had been too late when conveyed by the steam-vessels.

For several years, the extent and importance of our connexion with the United States had prompted the notion that there might be a more frequent and certain transit across the Atlantic, and the possibility of such an achievement was debated with all the ardour of scientific earnestness, and all the energy of commercial enterprise. Strange to say, the men of science, who, it might be supposed, should be best able to judge of so great an experiment, were to a man almost against it, while, as "the wish was," most probably, "father to the thought," the members of the mercantile community, and even some of the most cautious and hesitating, believed that the trial would be successful.

At length the great problem, on which so much depended, was brought to its solution. The Sirius, an admirably built vessel of seven hundred tons, with three hundred and twenty horse power, which had previously been engaged between London and Cork, sailed from the latter port on the 4th of

April, 1838, and struck boldly and directly across the ocean for New York. A few days after, the Great Western, a vessel noble in every way in her proportions and appointments, which had been built under the direction of a company of British merchants, started from Bristol for the same destination.

The voyage was triumphantly successful. The ships had been intended to stop at the Azores, Halifax, or St. John's, to shorten the voyage; but, without calling at a single port for assistance or supply, they held on their course towards America, and at length, on the 23rd of the same month, on the same day, the Sirius first, and the Great Western a few hours after, entered the harbour of New York. Long before their arrival notice of their coming had been given, and when the ships approached the shores of the greatest commercial city of the New World, they were greeted with flags and banners, and with music and ringing of bells, and the acclamations and applause of unnumbered multitudes.

Half the width of the Atlantic had been annihilated, the year had been doubled in its length, and three-fourths of the causes of strife and discord had been destroyed for ever; for ten thousand avenues had been opened of mutual advantage and regard between the two great branches of the most wealthy, the most enterprising, and the most powerful among the nations of the world.

Within two years afterwards, the Oriental Steam-packet Company placed their magnificent vessels on the waves of the Mediterranean, and brought the cities and the millions of India within the journey of a month. Again, and two years more saw a line of equally splendid ships bringing every fortnight the rich produce of our West India Colonies. A squadron of steamers have likewise commenced their errands of prosperity and peace beyond the isthmus of Panama, and even at the present moment a project is under the favourable consideration of Government for uniting the antipodes with Britain by saving the circuit of half the globe. And the whole of these vessels, be it remembered, perform their voyages with almost the punctual regularity of a mail-coach running between two neighbouring towns.

Although the tide of prosperity which had set in in favour of steam-navigation was interrupted for a while in 1841, when the unfortunate President was lost in its passage across the Atlantic, the enterprising spirit of the ship-building community was by no means checked, and in 1843, the Great Britain steam-ship was launched; this vessel was, however, doomed to almost a similar misfortune, having run ashore in Dundrum Bay in the autumn of 1846, and although all the passengers and crew were saved, and the vessel, after the lapse of several months, was, by a great engineering triumph, at length got off, the owners, nevertheless, did not think fit to trust it again to the mercy of the waves of the Atlantic.

THE GREAT BRITAIN IN DUNDRUM BAY.

THE SOUTH HETTON COLLIERIES RAILWAY—SHOWING HOW A TRAIN OF LOADED WAGGONS
DRAWS A TRAIN OF EMPTY ONES UP THE INCLINED PLANE.

THE RAILWAY.

HOW astonished would our forefathers be if they could
but see the changes England has undergone during
the last quarter of a century—if they could but
behold the contrast between the old lumbering stage-
wagon, and the rapid railway train, that rushes along
like the giant in his seven-league boots, and rivals all
the wonders of old romance. How they would stare to see
a long train thundering by at full speed, hissing and groaning,
like a monstrous serpent that was nearly cut asunder in fifty
places (for such, no doubt, to them would appear the spaces
between the carriages), and trying to outstrip the very pain it
seemed to writhe beneath. And how great would be their

surprise when they were told that that monster, with its red fiery mouth, shrieking as it flew past, was fed on fire, and shod with iron, and would go a mile a minute without once stopping (excepting to drink, when it swallowed scores of gallons at a draught), for a long summer's day—that it could leave the metropolis of England and reach the capital of Scotland in nine hours, while in their own time, less than an hundred years ago, in 1763, there was only a coach once a-month, which was twelve, and very often fourteen or fifteen days in journeying the same distance.

When we come to consider that at the above date coaches had been in use for something like a hundred years, we may suppose that they moved at a snail's pace indeed at the time they were first introduced, and supplanted the old system of travelling by pack-horses. Travellers then-a-days were routed out of bed before it was light, and found a string of forty or fifty horses, ready packed and saddled for the journey, stretching from one end to the other of the long narrow street of old-fashioned houses. After they had seated themselves, the procession moved forward, the tinkling bells of the leading horse guiding the others, who, following in his track, jolted their burdens over rugged stone causeways, or floundered with them knee-deep in the mire. How people travelled in those days may be gleaned from the complaint made by one who styled himself "a lover of his country," and in writing against the new-fangled notion of coaches, which he considered would be the ruin of trade, observed—" Before these coaches were set up, travellers rode on horseback, and men had boots, spurs, saddles, bridles, saddle-cloths, and good riding-suits. Most gentlemen, too, before they travelled in their coaches, used to ride with swords, belts, pistols, holsters, portmanteaus, and hat-cases; for when they rode on horseback, they rode in one suit and carried another to wear when they came to their journey's end, or lay by the way. And if they were women that travelled, they needed to have safeguards and hoods, side-saddles and pillions, with strappings, saddle or pillion cloths, which, for the most part, were either laced or embroidered."

For many years the old coaches were clumsy contrivances enough, and were always breaking down; while their speed was such, that Fielding tells us Parson Adams walked faster than they went in his days. An author, who wrote nearly two hundred years ago, in describing coach travelling, says—"We had nothing but mischief. Crack went one thing—bounce went another. 'Who-ho!' said Roger; then some one went all floundering in the mud. 'Oh! oh!' cried Miss. Scream, scream, went the maids. And this was the trade from morning to night." In these days, travellers were often forced to avail themselves of the still slower road-wagon, drawn by heavy cart-horses, or to journey to some neighbouring town by the old village carrier,

"Whose grey old tilted cart did oft appear
To move so slow, you'd think he never would get there."

By-and by, as the turnpike roads were improved, a lighter kind of coach came up, and with it a quicker rate of travelling; and in the course of the year 1784, the establishment of mail-coaches took place. Something like fifty years afterwards, coach-travelling reached its highest state of perfection; but seemingly only to give place to the railways—for at the time we write, there are not more than one or two mail-coaches running, throughout the kingdom. How railways came to be first of all introduced, and how they afterwards progressed until the enormous number of 3597 miles were opened for the purposes of passenger traffic, it will be our object to describe in the following pages.

Formerly, the whole of the fuel required for domestic consumption in this country was wood, which was abundantly supplied by the forests, which covered large tracts of land. For, of manufactures by any other means than manual labour there was, at this period, no thought. When coal was found, there were for a long time prejudices against its use; but when these ignorant objections had subsided, easier means of conveying it from the high regions beneath which it lies, were soon thought of. In the neighbourhood of Newcastle-upon-Tyne the produce of the mines began to be borne to vessels waiting in the river, by the laying down of pieces of wood upon the ground, end to end, for the wheels of the coal-wagons to run upon; just as, in the present day, labourers employed to wheel bricks and mortar for building, use boards for their barrows to pass over.

This was a tolerably old contrivance; for so long ago as 1680, Noger North, speaking of a Newcastle colliery, observes—"Another thing that is remarkable is their way-leaves; for when men have pieces of ground between the colliery and the river, they sell leave to lead coals over their ground, and so dear, that the owner of a rood of ground will expect £20 per annum for this leave. The manner of the carriage is by laying rails of timber, from the colliery down to the river, exactly straight and parallel; and bulky carts are made, with four rowlets fitting these rails, whereby the carriage is so easy, that one horse will draw down four or five chaldron of coals, and is an immense benefit to the coal-merchant."

The construction of these permanent ways, after great improvements had taken place on the first rude notion, was generally as follows:—In the first place, the ordinary track was rendered as level as possible, but generally with a little inclination towards one end. Upon this level road, pieces of wood, about six feet long and four or five inches square, were put crosswise at two or three feet from each other, and upon these were laid other pieces of wood, carefully sawn to about six or eight inches broad and five inches deep, which were placed at right angles with them, end to end, just so far apart as to allow of the wheels of the wagons to run upon them. These upper pieces were then pegged down to the lower ones, and the spaces between filled up with sand, stones, or any other substance. After a time, much inconvenience was felt from this system, for in the event of any one of the upper pieces becoming worn out or displaced, whether by the swelling

MOUTH OF COAL-PIT, BROSELY, SALOP.

of the soil from rain, or from any sudden shock, the whole of the way was necessarily interrupted until another piece was put into its place. This suggested what proved to be a very great improvement, for other pieces were placed longitudinally throughout the whole track, and fastened by pegs or screws, so that where one was injured it could within an hour be taken out and replaced, without injury to the rest. A farther advantage was obtained in the greater depth of gravel or ballast, as it is called, that could be used, and whereby the sleepers were protected from injury from the feet of the horses employed to drag the wagons

The wagons used to carry the coals on these railways usually held from two to three or four tons, and were drawn by one horse each, going upon small wheels; to which shortly afterwards the flange or projecting rim was attached to keep them in the track, and thus a rude outline of the whole principle of the railway was complete. But a difficulty was experienced at particular points in the roads, where there was either a steep ascent or a sharp turning; and as it was advantageous to keep the labour of the horse as equably engaged as possible, a plan was adopted, about the year 1716, of nailing thin plates of iron upon the surface of the rails, which by its greater smoothness offered less obstruction to the tire of the wheels, so that a horse could travel with a full load all the way with more ease, and get over these points with little difficulty.

From 1716 till fifty years afterwards, these were all the improvements effected in the rail, or tram-ways, as they were at that time more generally termed. Stone ways had indeed in some cases been formed, instead of wooden ones, but the surface was rougher, and they soon fell into disuse. A suggestion, however, was made about the year 1767, which was a great step in a forward direction. At the Colebrook Dale Iron-works, in Shropshire, there was a wooden railway for the general convenience of the concern, which, like all others, required frequent repairs; these also were often expensive, and had to be made at inconvenient periods. At a particular time, iron happened to be so low in price that it was hardly worth making; and several of the masters in consequence suffered their furnaces to go out. But the bringing a furnace again into work is a troublesome and expensive business, and Mr. Reynolds, one of the proprietors of the Colebrook Dale Works, who is celebrated as having been the first individual that ever set up an iron bridge in England, suggested the casting their pigs of iron into somewhat larger lengths than usual, and laying them down on the surface of the wooden rails of their tram-way; observing that when the price of the metal rose they could easily take them up and dispose of them. This, however, never was done, nor were the scantlings, as they were called, ever removed until they were replaced by the improved iron rail which afterwards came into use.

IRON-WORKS, COLEBROOK DALE.

These scantlings, it should be remarked, were only plain surfaces, and a gentleman of the name of Woodhouse, with a view to keep the carriages better in their track, suggested the formation of rails with hollow surfaces, something like the gutters in the streets of London. These were made to take a firm position in the ground by being cast broader at the bottom than the top, while they were also lighter and less expensive than they would have been, from having two apertures through their whole length. This kind of rail was certainly better than the last; but was never generally adopted.

Some five or six years after the iron scantlings were laid down at Colebrook Dale, the chief feature of the railway, as we now have it, was brought into use at one of the Duke of Norfolk's collieries near Sheffield. This was the flange or projecting ledge. It is true that the flange in that instance was placed on the rail instead of the wheel, but when once the advantage of using it was perceived, the best mode of applying it was sure to be speedily discovered, and the necessity for keeping the rail of a certain width, would at the same time force itself on the notice of those who were chiefly interested in the improvement of the railway. But it was several years after this improvement before it was generally adopted by the owners of iron-works and collieries. The first edge railway of which we have any account was laid down in the year 1801, at Lord Penrhyn's slate quarries in Wales. It was composed of pieces four feet six inches in length, each of which was, with the end of the piece that joined it, fitted into an iron block firmly embedded in the road. In order to keep the wheels in their places, they were made with a grooved tire, but this in the course of time was found to wear away and to make the carriage *drag*, and Mr. Watt, the inventor, in order to remedy the defect, adopted the method of putting a regular flange on each side of the wheel, thus giving both to the rail and the wheel a flat surface; and such was the advantage of his plan, that two horses could draw a train of as many as twenty-four wagons, each of which contained a ton weight of material; and no more than ten horses were required to do the work which it had formerly required four hundred to perform.

The benefit arising from the use of edge rails was so apparent that they came into general use; but it was soon perceived that two flanges to the wheel were unnecessary, for by retaining the one on the inner edge of the tire, it was evident that the carriage could not be thrown off the rail (except through the impulse of some extraordinary violence), which would doubtless produce the same effect even if the wheel had two flanges. This form of wheel has been in use ever since.

With regard to the rails, there have been various changes, as, for instance, some have been cast with the thickness greater in the middle than at the ends, so that whilst the latter rested on the *chairs*, the middle might rest on the solid ground. These are called *fish-bellied* rails, and have been laid down on many lines; but the rail most commonly in use is that called the *longitudinal*, which is of the same thickness throughout its whole length, and the general weight of which is about seventy-five pounds to the yard.

On account of the expense, these rails were, with few exceptions, for a long time made of cast iron, which was, from its brittle nature, very liable to be broken (though of course much more durable than wood); but so long as only low rates of speed were required, this was of comparatively little consequence. But when railways came into common use for the conveyance of passengers, and a speed of from fifteen to twenty miles an hour was required, stoppages for repairs were found to be of serious moment, and malleable iron was in several instances used. Still the cost was a serious impediment to its general adoption, till the invention by Mr. Birkenshawe of a cheap method of rolling iron into bars for rails and other purposes.

As we have seen, when railways were first adopted, animal power was the only means employed for moving the carriages; but when their advantages had become so apparent, as was the case soon after they became common, it was rightly conceived that the steam-engine might be made available for the purpose, and Captain Trevithick, one of those enterprising and able individuals whose skill and ability have been nurtured in the mines of Cornwall, adapted the steam-engine for locomotive purposes. Something of the same plan had been suggested in the patents of Watt in 1784, but it was not complete, and in 1802, Messrs. Trevithick and Vivian took out a patent for a high-pressure steam-carriage, after the model of which they built several others in the course of a few years, and one of which

was tried in 1805, on a tramway at Merthyr Tydvil, and drew
a train containing ten tons of iron, besides several passengers.

It was a singular, but not an unnatural mistake, after the
experience that had been obtained for the traction of carriages
on railways by animal power, that when great weights were to
be moved by mechanical agency alone, the wheels of the
carriages would not bite close enough upon the edges of the
rails to move onwards at the self-same time. It was supposed
that although there could be no doubt of the engines causing
the wheels to revolve, yet they would not turn round precisely
in the same place. Above all, it was thought self-evident that
if they did move forward on a perfect level, the slightest ascent
would suffice to stop their tractive action. We have, however,
lived to learn that no more erroneous idea could have been
entertained; for comparatively steep inclined planes are now
daily surmounted by railway engines.

To obviate the supposed defect of an insufficient adhesion
of the wheels to the rails, a Mr. Blenkinsop took out a patent
for a machine to move a large cog-wheel, the projections of
which fitted into a rack made to correspond, and which was
laid down alongside the railway. This plan was adopted, and
worked many years, on the Hunslet Moor Collieries' tramway,
near Leeds. The reader may see, as we have done, this curious
relic, the notched rack; for it yet remains on the Moor—the
gibe of many a passer-by.

The advantages of railway communication had been for
years growing upon the public mind, and at length its importance became so strongly impressed upon the inhabitants of
Manchester and the merchants of its great port, Liverpool,
that they determined not to be left behind in the race of improvement, and accordingly applied to Parliament for power to
construct a railway between the two towns.

An Act, conferring the necessary powers, was obtained
in 1825, at a time when excessive commercial activity had

given a fresh stimulus to their exertions; and although a period of more than corresponding depression and distress immediately followed, they carried out their design. To accomplish the formation of this railway, the engineer had almost every variety of difficulty to contend with. He had hills to surmount, flats to pass, and, what was worse than all, one of those loose morasses to make firm, which are not unfrequent in the north of England, but which had to be made as solid as the common ground before it would be able to sustain the ponderous weights which would have to pass over it. Chat Moss was notorious as one of the most dangerous and uncertain quagmires in the kingdom. Whether the instability of the ground for so many miles was owing to the filtering of the waves from the Irish Sea, or from the settling of the waters from the heights of Cumberland and Westmoreland, was, and is still, a problem. Many plans were followed, which proved unsuccessful; but at length the engineer of the new railway decided upon throwing in bundles of "kids" or faggots, till at last a broad foundation, of floating basis, was established, and as the workmen wrought higher and higher, the way gained hourly in solid character, and in the end, when the ballast for the rail was laid, a road, firm, substantial, and enduring, was formed of the most fragile material upon which engineer could lay his hand.

A viaduct, or elevated roadway, over Sankey Valley was another difficult task. For the security of the work, it was necessary to drive two hundred piles, varying from twenty to thirty feet in length, into the foundation of each of the ten piers. Thus, in all, two thousand piles had to be driven; and all those who have seen the pile-driving engine at work, and noticed the small progress made at each blow from the ponderous monkey, will have some idea of the labour and tedious nature of the task.

This railway was completed in 1830, and the month of October in the following year was fixed for its being opened.

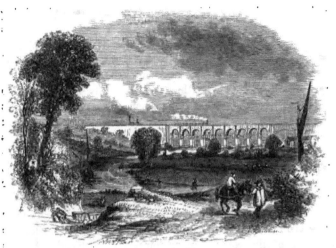

SANKEY VIADUCT.

for the use of the public. For some time before, there had
been much debate among the directors as to the means that
should be used for drawing the carriages, and a strong feeling
existed in favour of employing stationary steam-engines, which
should work ropes to and fro, at certain intervals, along the
line. Horse power being evidently insufficient to keep up the
speed which the directors and the public desired to attain, it
was ultimately decided upon using locomotives, and the directors offered a premium of £500 for the best that could be
produced with certain conditions. These were that the chimney
should emit no smoke, that the engine should be on springs,
not weigh more than six tons, or four tons and a half if it had
only four wheels, that it should be able to draw three times its
own weight, and not cost more than £550.

Four engines with the required qualifications were produced
on the day of trial. Of these one was withdrawn. Of the
others, the first was the Novelty, constructed by Messrs. Braith-

waite and Ericson, which was of a singular construction, being made exceedingly light, and its draft being produced by means of a blowing machine. The next was the Rocket, built by Mr. R. Stephenson and Mr. Booth, one of the directors. The third was called the Sanspareil, and was built by Mr. Hackworth much on the principle of Trevithick's engine, only having two cylinders instead of one. The performance of the first was very promising, until an accident prevented its further progress; the last drew a load of nineteen tons at the rate of fifteen miles an hour, but it was also disabled by an accident; and Mr. Stephenson's engine accordingly gained the prize, but not without deserving it, for it accomplished more than had been either required or contemplated.

The line was opened for traffic shortly afterwards, with much ceremony, all the great ministers of state and the leading men of the country being present. Although the success of the Stockton and Darlington railway had in some degree prepared the public for the benefits that would be derived from that between Manchester and Liverpool, yet when it was fairly in play, they exceeded all that the most sanguine expectations could have anticipated.

The eminent advantages which had resulted from the Liverpool and Manchester railway, suggested the idea of the still greater benefit that might be obtained by uniting the metropolis with one of the great manufacturing cities; and Mr. Robert Stephenson was engaged to lay out and construct a line for that purpose between Birmingham and London. Few great undertakings ever excited so much controversy as this. The distance to be traversed was a hundred and ten miles. Lofty heights had to be surmounted, rivers to be crossed, deep valleys and ravines to be passed, and almost every difficulty that can be opposed to engineering skill had to be overcome. But the spirited proprietors, and the able engineers engaged upon it, persevered; and, the Act of Parliament having been obtained, one by one the several obstacles were overcome; and the great emporium, so often called the "toy-shop of Europe," was united to the metropolis of the world.

The capital expended on the Liverpool and Manchester railway had been upwards of a million and a half; that laid out on the London and Birmingham line, was more than seven millions and a quarter: and even that was destined to be exceeded by other projects of equal extent and of equal importance, for next came the design of uniting the old metropolis of the commerce of the Western Ocean, Bristol, with London. One of the most striking of the many engineering difficulties that had to be surmounted in the construction of this line, was the excavation through the solid rock of the celebrated Box

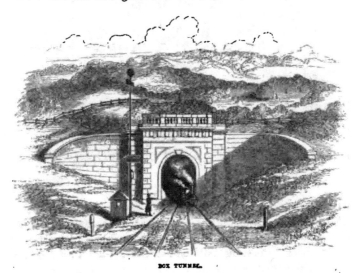

BOX TUNNEL.

Tunnel, which was satisfactorily accomplished under the direction of Mr. Brunel, the chief engineer. This tunnel, which is ventilated by six shafts, varying from 70 to 300 feet in depth,

is 3175 yards in length. The accomplishment of this undertaking was regarded in the light of a great engineering
triumph; and, compared with it, the minor achievements
of "cuttings" through the high grounds, and the raising of
embankments along the valleys, of which there were several
of great extent on this line, though laborious undertakings
enough of themselves, sink almost into insignificance. By

RAILWAY EMBANKMENT NEAR BATH.

the genius of Mr. Lock, the line between the banks of the
Thames and Southampton has been rendered so safe, so speedy
in transit, and so convenient, that the state dues of the latter
place, which before the railway was made were only a few
hundred thousand pounds, have now increased to upwards of
four millions per annum, and it has become the third port
in the kingdom, and head-quarters for the highway between
Britain and the Southern World,

194

From this point the commercial activity of capitalists has been proceeding, till all the great lines of communication have been supplied with railways, and the making of them has become the greatest business that has ever been followed in this or any other country; and it is now evident that Britain will speedily be mapped by a network of railways for the speedy intercourse of her different communities.

To show how immense is the business of forming railroads, it is only necessary to state, that while the capital invested in the first of our staple manufactures, the cotton trade, is about £40,000,000, that in our woollen trade may be estimated at from £18,000,000, that in our iron trade at about £12,000,000, that in our silk business at less than £16,000,000, that in our railroads is upwards of £100,000,000. One of the largest fortunes that has ever been made was acquired by one individual who, the other day, was engaged in the comparatively insignificant business of a draper at York, and has now at his command the services, and in his hands the interest and the welfare, of upwards of 50,000 labourers, and has created a fortune (for the manner in which it has been realized) unparalleled in the history of the world.

In conclusion, it may be useful to record the following quotation from an article published in the *Quarterly Review*, very little more than twenty years since, which shows the folly of a too hasty condemnation of an invention then on the eve of developing itself in its gigantic strength. The reviewer observed:—"As to those persons who speculate on the making railways generally throughout the kingdom, and superseding all the canals, all the wagons, mail and stage coaches, postchaises, and, in short, every other mode of conveyance by land and by water, we deem them and their visionary schemes unworthy of notice;" and in allusion to an opinion expressed of the probability of railway engines running at the rate of eighteen miles an hour, on a railway then in contemplation between London and Woolwich, the reviewer adds—"We should as soon expect the people of Woolwich to suffer themselves to be fired off upon one of Congreve's ricochet rockets, as trust themselves to the mercy of a machine going at such a rate." In two-and-twenty years afterwards, trains running at more than double this speed had become of daily occurrence, and nearly quadruple the speed which so alarmed the reviewer had been attained with perfect safety.

RAILWAY CUTTING.

GAS-LIGHT.

WHAT the dark wintry nights in England were some centuries ago, may be imagined from the circumstance that there were, with but few exceptions, no common high-ways as now; and that the cresset which blazed at the top of the windy and hilly street, or the beacon-light that flashed high up on the tall and embattled turret, above donjon-keep, and bar-bican, and drawbridge, and threw its crimson glare upon the dark waters of the sur-rounding moat, were the only signals that warned alike

both serf and freed-man to rush to the rescue of their feudal lord, when forest outlaws, or mail-clad marauders in the service of some neighbouring hostile baron, assailed the chieftain's stronghold. Over marsh and moorland, and a wild wilderness of forest, the midnight beacon would blaze, startling the darkness by its lurid glare, awakening the swineherd in his hut, the hunter on his heather couch, the gosherd beside the fen, the yeoman in his moated grange, the archer in his thatched hovel, and the fisherman beside the lonely mere; while the bell of the distant abbey aroused the shaven priest, for the monk to pray and the layman to fight, until either the castle was stormed, or the assailants driven off. In these and in far later times, the solitary beacon that gleamed high above the tall headlands which surround our sea-girt coast, served to alarm our island against an invasion on the part of foreign foes. And many an old man still living can remember the period when, even in populous cities and towns, only a little oil-lamp stood blinking and winking here and there, which on stormy nights was often extinguished, leaving the streets in perfect darkness.

When the streets were unlighted, the old watchman went his nightly rounds, with his long sharp halbert in one hand and his lantern in the other, calling out, "Lantern and a whole candle! Hang out your lights!"—for this was the way many of the London streets were lighted about four hundred years ago, there being a law which compelled a certain number of householders in each street to hang out lanterns with "a whole candle" during the dark nights; and the old watchman thundered at the doors of those who neglected to do so. In Queen Mary's days the watchman had a bell, which he rung at the end of the street every time he passed. Only one hundred years ago, London was so badly watched and lighted, that the Lord Mayor and Aldermen went with a petition to the King, stating that the city was so infested at night by gangs of lawless men, armed with "bludgeons, pistols, cut-lasses," and other weapons, that it was dangerous to go out after dusk, as so many were robbed, wounded, and often murdered. While this was the case in the capital, one may imagine how unprotected the provinces remained. This, it must be remembered, was the age of foot-pads and highway-men. Before the doors of some of the old houses in London, there is still to be seen, on each side of the posts of the arched iron lamp-rail, an extinguisher, shaped like the old post-boy's horn; this was to thrust the torches or flambeaus in, to extinguish them, after the inmates of the house had been lighted home. Link-boys, or torch-bearers, were as common then as street-sweepers are in the present day, and picked up what they could by lighting passengers along the streets. Then came the age of oil-lamps, about 1762, and we had the lamp-lighter, with his ladder, oil-can, and cotton wicks, and with tow around his wrist, trimming and cleaning in the day-time; and in the dusk of evening climbing the posts, and "lighting-up." Then the bold robbers, who carried "pistols, bludgeons, and blunderbusses," began to quit the cities, and to plunder passengers on the highways—for they "loved darkness rather than light." The discovery of Gas, and the application of it for the purpose of lighting our chief towns and cities by night, no doubt did as much good towards checking street robberies as the organisation of the powerful Police-force.

Tenanting as we do a world which is placed as much under the dominion of darkness as of light, without the assistance of artificial light, man's labour would always be checked, and his efforts at improvement after sunset rendered, in many instances, useless. Human observation was, therefore, naturally directed, in the earliest ages, to the most enduring means of procuring this great requisite of agreeable and useful existence. Fatty substances, with a wick inserted in their mass, were used instead of the lighted pine or faggot. But with this invention the improvement of artificial light was stationary for ages. It was not even until towards the middle of the last century that the first clear discovery was made of the present brilliant means of procuring artificial light.

All the different substances which have been used, from the earliest times, for this purpose, have actually been resolved into gas before they underwent the process of combustion. But this fact was unknown until the grand discoveries in chemistry unfolded the properties of the aërial bodies. The fact of inflammable gases constituting the means of light in bitumen and pit-coal, seems first to have been practically observed by a clergyman.

The Rev. Mr. Clayton, in a memoir published in the "Transactions of the Royal Society," in 1739, gives the following very interesting account of his experiments, which furnish the earliest evidence of the possibility of extracting from coal, by means of heat, a permanently elastic fluid of an inflammable nature.

"Having introduced a quantity of coal into a retort, and placed it over an open fire, at first there came over only phlegm, and afterwards a black oil, and then likewise a spirit arose which I could noways condense; but it forced my lute (the clay employed to close the seams of the retort), or broke my glasses. Once, when it had forced my lute, coming close thereto in order to repair it, I observed that the spirit which issued out caught fire at the flame of the candle, and continued burning with violence as it issued out in a steam, which I blew out and lighted alternately for several times. I then had a mind to try if I could save any of this spirit; in order to do this. I took a turbinated receiver, and putting a candle to the pipe of the receiver whilst the spirit rose, I observed that it catched flame, and continued burning at the end of the pipe, though you could not observe what fed the flame. I then blew it out and lighted it again several times; after which I fixed a bladder, squeezed and void of air, to the pipe of the receiver. The oil and flame descended into the receiver, but the spirit still ascending, blew up the bladder. I then filled a good many bladders therewith, and might have filled an inconceivable number more; for the spirit continued to run for several hours, and filled the bladders almost as fast as a man could have blown them with his mouth; and yet the quantity of coals distilled was inconsiderable.

"I kept this spirit in the bladders a considerable time, and endeavoured several ways to condense it, but in vain; and when I had a mind to divert strangers or friends, I have frequently taken one of these bladders, and pricked a hole therein with a pin, and compressing gently the bladder near the flame of a candle till it once took fire, it would then continue flaming till all the spirit was compressed out of the bladder; which was the more surprising, because no one could discern any difference in the appearance between this bladder and those which are filled with common air."

Mr. Murdoch, of Redruth, in Cornwall, in 1792, seems to have been the first who thought of applying this discovery to any practical purpose. He commenced a series of experiments upon the properties of the gasses contained in different substances, such as peat, wood, and coal; and it occurred to him that by confining the gases in proper vessels, and afterwards expelling them through pipes, they might be employed as a convenient and economical substitute for lamps and candles.

At length, in 1798, Mr. Murdoch publicly exhibited the results of his matured plans, by constructing an apparatus for lighting the Soho Foundry, Birmingham, with suitable arrangements for the purification of the gas. These experiments, Dr. Henry states, "were continued with occasional interruptions until the peace of 1802, when the illumination of the Soho manufactory afforded an opportunity of making public display of the new lights; and they were made to constitute a principal feature in that exhibition."

In the course of the years 1803 and 1804, the Lyceum Theatre, in London, was lighted with gas, under the direction of Mr. Winsor; and in 1804 and 1805, Mr. Murdoch had an opportunity of carrying his plans into effect on a larger scale, by means of the apparatus erected under his superintendence in the extensive cotton-mills of Messrs. Philipps and Son, of Manchester.

The French have claimed the priority in the exhibition of gas-light; but the earliest display of it in that country did not take place till 1802, when it was exhibited in Paris. It has already been shown that Mr. Murdoch's exhibition of it was earlier, by several years.

From the first lighting up of Boulton and Watts's Soho Foundry by gas, in 1802, to the close of 1822, a period of only twenty years, so rapidly had the discovery proceeded, and so high was the appreciation of it by the public, that, by the report of Sir William Congreve, it appears that the capital vested in the gas-works of the metropolis alone amounted to one million sterling, while the pipes connected with the various establishments, embraced an extent of upwards of one hundred and fifty miles. In the course of a few years after it was first introduced it was, indeed, adopted by all the principal towns in the kingdom, for lighting streets, as well as shops and public buildings. Into private dwellings, through the careless and imperfect way in which the service-pipes were at first fitted up, and which occasioned annoyances, it was more slowly received. But as a better knowledge of its management has been acquired, it has come into more general use, till, now, gas is employed in every quarter where the means of obtaining it are within reach.

The apparatus for the production and purification of coal-gas, consist, in the first place, of the *retorts*, or vessels for decomposing by heat the coal from which the gas is to be procured; secondly, of the *dip-pipes* and *condensing main*, employed to conduct the gas into vessels, where it is removed from the tar and other gross products that come over the gas and tend to impair the brilliancy of the light; thirdly, of the purifying apparatus, for abstracting the sulphuretted hydrogen, carbonic acid, &c., by which the gas is contaminated; and lastly, of the *gasometer*, or gas-holder, with its tank, into which the gas is finally received in a purified state.

The *retorts* are usually formed of cast iron, and are commonly of a cylindrical shape. They are fixed in brick-work, with furnaces beneath them. The fuel required for carbonizing a given quantity of coal, that is, for separating the gaseous matter from it, is in general about two-fifths of its weight. The bright red heat is the most favourable to the process. The quality of the gas, yielded by coal, varies greatly at different periods of the heating operation. If the coal has not been previously well dried, scarcely any other than aqueous vapours and carbonic acid will, at first, be given off; these will be succeeded by the gases required for use, light carburetted hydrogen and olefiant gas, together with sulphuretted hydrogen; and these will gradually diminish in quantity till towards the close of the process, when almost the only products will be carbonic oxide and hydrogen. The time which elapses from the period at which the retorts are *charged*, or fitted, to the moment when they are *drawn*, or emptied of the residuary carbon, or cinder, varies with the kind of coal used: cannel coal, which is easily decomposed, requires but three and a half or four hours, while Newcastle coal takes six. The quantity of gas also varies with the quality of coal: this cannel coal yields 430 cubic feet of gas per hundredweight; Newcastle coal, about 370 feet.

The *dip-pipes* are bent pipes from which the gas ascends out of the retorts, as it is produced, into the *condensing main*, a large cast-iron pipe placed in a horizontal position, and supported by columns in front of the brickwork which contains the retorts. The tar, aqueous vapour, and oleaginous matter, which ascend with the gas from the retort, are left by it in the condensing main; though it is difficult to prevent small portions of these substances from escaping with it.

The further purification of the gas has now to be effected; and after passing from the condensing main, it is conveyed by pipes into other apparatus for perfecting its purification. Olefiant gas and light carburetted hydrogen, the two compounds of carbon and hydrogen, which it is sought to obtain, are mixed with several deleterious substances which the coal yields, together with them, during its destructive distillation by heat. In small quantity, carbonic oxide, nitrogen, and hydrogen, come off; but in larger, carbonic acid and sulphuretted hydrogen. These last two are the most objectionable for impurity, and can, fortunately, be more easily separated from the gas than the others.

Quick-lime, being a substance with which carbonic acid and sulphuretted hydrogen will easily unite, is employed, in one form or other, in all gas establishments, for the last step of the purifying process to which coal-gas is submitted to render it fit for combustion. Sometimes the cream of lime, or lime slaked with a little more than the usual quantity of water, is employed, and then it is necessary to agitate the liquid so as to assist the gas to come into contact with fresh portions of the lime; and in other establishments dry lime is used. In very large establishments, the gas is forced in succession through a series of vessels stored with lime, in order to purify it thoroughly; in others, an apparatus is affixed for supplying fresh lime as often as the old material has become so saturated with the deleterious gases as to be unfit for use. Being freed from impurity, it is next conveyed into the large vessel in which it is stored up for use.

The *gasometer* is an inverted cylindrical cup, of which the diameter is about double the depth. It is constructed of sheet iron, well rivetted at the joints, and kept in shape by stays and braces of cast or bar iron. The sheets of iron are made to overlap at the joints, and a slip of canvas well-besmeared with white-lead is interposed between the lappings, to secure perfect tightness. The gasometer is suspended in a tank containing water, by a chain and counterpoise, over pullies. As the gasometer, when immersed, suffers a loss of weight equal to that of the portion of fluid it displaces, arrangement has to be made to counteract the varying pressure resulting from the different depths to which it is immersed, or the gas in it will be expelled at different times with varying force. It is easy, however, to calculate this force, and provide against it.

Under the bottom of the tank in which the gasometer floats, the gas is introduced and conducted off by pipes. As these pipes are usually below the level of those in the street with which they communicate, they are, apt to be filled up with condensed water, which passes off in a vaporous state with the gas. Vessels for receiving the condensed water are, therefore, connected with the entrance and exit pipes, and so contrived that the accumulated water can be easily removed.

The transmission of the gas for use, from the gasometer, is through the main and service pipes—the size of the former being relative to the united sizes of the latter; that is, the sum of the areas of the sections of main-pipes being equal to the sum of the areas of the sections of branch or service pipes supplied. The supply of gas to the main-pipe is regulated by the "governor," a piece of mechanism consisting of a rod and valve placed between them and the pipe by which the gas enters the gasometer. The main-pipes are usually of cast iron; the sections of about three yards in length, being joined by sockets, which are caulked with gasket, and soldered with lead. Water in vapour carried off by the gas will be condensed in the main-pipes, and, therefore, in laying them, it is necessary to observe a declivity towards points where there can be drainers to discharge the water. Neglect in taking the levels, so as to obtain the proper drainage, often occasions the pipes to be taken up, an annoyance that might, in most cases, have been avoided. The service-pipes are usually of block-tin, as being more durable than copper or other metal that would be likely to be selected. A proper inclination for draining these pipes should also be observed in placing them, or the condensed water which collects in them, will cause the lights to flicker, and, at times, will extinguish them. The soldering should also be carefully performed, as lead dropped into the pipes often prevents the passage of the gas.

The advantages of coal-gas over every other means of artificial light at present in use are very generally acknowledged. Its cheapness is one of its greatest recommendations; and it is liable to but little fluctuation in price, while wax, tallow, and oil, depending on supplies more or less precarious, are liable to become very dear in the market. Assuming that 1 lb. of tallow candles cost nine-pence, and will burn 40 hours; that a gallon of oil costs two shillings, and will yield light equal to 600 candles for one hour; that wax is three times as expensive as tallow; and that 1000 cubic feet of coal-gas costs nine shillings; we may state the relative cost of the same degree of illumination from these different substanstances, after making suitable allowance for waste, wicks, &c., to be as follows—wax 100, tallow 25, oil 5, gas 3.

We may observe in conclusion, that light from coal-gas is not only more cheap, but is also more convenient for most purposes than the light yielded by other substances. Without gas, too, many of our manufactures would be bereft of the steady and powerful lights they require so absolutely, and which can be brought near to them without danger by means of flexible pipes. Gas-light is, in a word, one of the great accessories necessary to our present advanced and advancing civilization; and if its splendour, displayed in so many beautifully fanciful jets and burners, were to be abstracted from our places of public assembly, and its safety and convenience were to be replaced in our streets by the dull groping demi-darkness of the old oil-lamps—but for one year—there is little doubt but it would considerably put back the state of art and science, and of the general business of mankind.

When the rapid advances made by science are taken into consideration, we are not hazarding an impossible opinion in stating that a few years may possibly supplant the general use of gas as a means of street illumination, as this has already supplanted the old system of oil-lamps; for a new light, which is only surpassed by that of the sun, has been produced by electricity, and ere long the streets of our cities will probably be lighted up at midnight, by its agency, almost as vividly as if the noon-day sun shone down upon them.

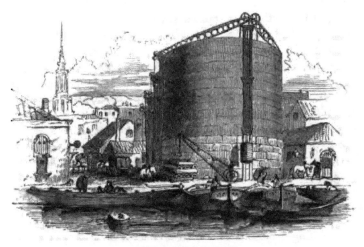

THE CITY OF LONDON GAS-WORKS.

117.

THE ELECTRIC TELEGRAPH.

S quick as thought is an old mode of expression, used to convey an idea of the greatest rapidity: but no one, until lately, ever dreamed that a thought could be sent hundreds of miles in a few seconds; and that a person standing in London might hold a conversation with another in Edinburgh, put questions and receive answers, just as if they were seated together in one room, instead of being three hundred miles apart. The Electric Telegraph is another of the wonderful discoveries of modern times.

The robber gets into the train with his plunder, miles away from London, and quite chuckles with delight to think how rapidly he is flying from all pursuit, and how soon he shall be buried in the heart of that great city, where all search for him will be useless.

The express train rushes along. It has already traversed nearly one hundred miles in two hours; another hour, and he will be in London; and at the thought, he clutches the booty with delight—for he knows not that just at that moment tidings of the robbery has reached the railway station he had left so far behind; that he had been seen in the neighbourhood where the robbery was committed; and that a messenger, with the rapidity of lightning, was travelling along those wires, that had already rung a little bell in the telegraph office in London, and was now telling the London policemen what had been stolen, describing also his very person, and the carriage in which he was riding. And all this immense distance had been traversed by the messenger, and the tidings delivered, in the space of a few seconds—even while the express train, with all its speed, had advanced but little more than a mile.

Then, when the robber would leap gladly out of the carriage, and chuckle at his clever escape, and think how soon a cab would carry him to the place where he could turn his stolen goods into cash, a policeman, who had been waiting for him some time, would step up, seize him by the collar, order his luggage to be opened, and there would be found the booty; while the thief, who stood pale, silent, and horror-stricken, would be dragged off to jail, tried, and transported.

Such is one of the wonders performed by the electric telegraph; and it has in many similar instances proved itself the most valuable assistant of Justice that ever stepped in to the aid of the Law.

Upon such an important discovery, it is almost impossible to write calmly—for the instantaneous transmission of thought from one corner of a kingdom to another, by means of a piece of wire, would have been pronounced, but a few years ago, a fiction only fitted for a tale to be bound up with Baron Munchausen. If wires were placed around the earth, Puck's promise, in Shakspere, might be fulfilled in a less number of seconds than he boasted of minutes, in sending a message round the world. Like many other inventions, however, which had been set down for romantic projects, it had, nevertheless, long been earnestly considered a possible achievement, by a few scientific minds. Its eventual discovery sprung from no sudden and happy idea, but from prolonged and persevering application.

Some fantastic displays of electric phenomena, after Franklin's well-known experiment with the kite, seem first to have drawn the attention of philosophers to the possibility of employing electricity as a means of human communication at great dis-

119

tances. Lomond, in 1787, made some practical approaches to such a discovery; but Reizer, in 1794, succeeded in constructing a servicable telegraph, though its value was little compared with those now in use. Wire was the conductor, as in the present telegraphs, but the electric spark, elicited by friction, was the only agent. The wire conducted to a darkened room, around which were placed pieces of tin-foil inscribed with letters, and fixed on plates of glass. The spark, it was found, in leaping across the glass plates to pursue its course along the wire, would illuminate the pieces of tin-foil, and thus the letters could be read.

Volta's discovery of the direction of an electric current by means of the battery which bears his name, and the discovery of the decomposition of water by it, by Nicholson and Carlisle, in 1800, gave a new turn to the project; and in 1807, Sömmering, of Munich, invented a telegraph for which he employed the battery—including the principle of the decomposition of water.

Ronalds, of Hamersmith, in 1816, recurred to the frictional electricity, or spark, and not only invented an improved telegraph, but an electric clock: the latter invention had been realized, also, by Buzengeiger, in Germany, the year before.

In 1819, Professor Œrsted, of Copenhagen, made his great discovery of the action of a galvanic current upon a magnetic needle. He observed that when a galvanic current passes along a wire, placed parallel and near to a magnetic needle, free to turn on its centre, the needle is deflected to one side or the other, according to the direction in which the current is transmitted. A single wire has but small power on the needle; but Professor Schweiger invented the "multiplier," as he called it, in which the needle, being surrounded with many successive coils of insulated wire, is acted upon by the joint force of all. Another important discovery was made shortly after, by Œrsted, Davy, Arago, and others. They succeeded in rendering iron magnetic, by the passage of a galvanic current through a wire coiled round the iron. It was found that, providing the iron to be magnetized were perfectly soft and pure, the magnetic property remained only during the actual transmission of the electricity, and was lost immediately on the interruption of the electric circuit. If the iron to be exposed to the influence of the galvanic current, were combined with sulphur, carbon, or phosphorus, the magnetic power became, to a greater or lesser extent, permanent in it.

These discoveries, chiefly of Œrsted, form the basis of the invention of the electric telegraphs now in use; but it is to two other intelligent individuals that we owe the application of these discoveries in our own country.

Mr. Cooke, having witnessed some experiments of Professor Moencke's, at Heidelberg, applied himself to the prosecution of a scheme for conveying intelligence by electricity; and during 1836 he was engaged in the construction of telegraphic instruments, and in attempting to bring them into use on some of our northern railways. In the beginning of 1837, he became acquainted with Professor Wheatstone, who had been attending to the same subject of invention; and in June, of the same year, they took out a patent for a telegraph, conjointly. The principal points of novelty in this invention were, the use of a much smaller number of needles to denote all the required signals, than in the telegraphs hitherto constructed; the employment of the temporary magnetism, excited by the current, in soft iron, to ring an alarm, either directly or indirectly, by suitable machinery; and the reciprocal arrangement by which the invention was rendered applicable to a long line of communication. At one terminus, five needles were arranged with their axes in a horizontal line. When at rest these needles hung vertically, by reason of a slight preponderance given to their lower ends. At the other terminus five pairs of finger-keys, resembling those of a piano-forte, were placed over a trough of mercury, to which a voltaic battery was attached.

On depressing the keys, the wires belonging to them, respectively, were brought into connexion with the trough. The wires receiving the magnetic current, it flowed along them with the rapidity of lightning, and caused the needles to deflect at the other terminus. Letters were indicated by the movement of the needles, and a communication could thus be carried on rapidly and with certainty. It should also be observed, that the instruments at the two termini were rendered reciprocating; a set of finger-keys and a voltaic battery being placed at each station, so that either could transmit or receive a signal. The bell or alarum, rung to draw attention at either terminus, was of two kinds; a hammer was impelled against the bell by magnetic attraction, or a catch was released from a train of clock-work, which, by the usual intervention of a wheel and pallets, rang the bell, as in common alarums.

In the beginning of 1838, Messrs. Cooke and Wheatstone obtained a patent for improvements which rendered it possible, not merely for the two extreme termini, but for any number of intermediate stations, to hold communication. The five needles were now reduced to two; and some important improvements made in insulating and protecting the wires, which were to be laid beneath the earth, in tubes of wood, iron, or earthenware.

In 1839, this improved telegraph was brought into actual operation on the Great Western Railway, and the inventors were gratified by seeing their scheme triumphantly successful.

Other discoverers were in the field, as well as our two meritorious countrymen. Dr. Steinbeil, of Munich, substituted for the ordinary voltaic battery the magneto-electric machine, in which, according to Faraday's great discovery, the electric current was derived by induction from a permanent magnet. He also contrived an apparatus by which, instead of merely indicating letters, the needle could be made drop ink on paper, so that, from the number and arrangement of the dots, a communication could be fixed on a strip and afterwards read. The objection to this latter invention, was the slowness of the communication so made. Professor Morse, of America, also turned his attention towards making the electric telegraph a registering instrument. In his scheme a pencil was, at first, substituted for ink; but the pencil being found to require such frequent pointing, from breakage, was removed for a steel point, which pressed the paper into a groove, and made an indentation. From the number of these marks various letters and figures were to be denoted.

In the beginning of 1840, Professor Wheatstone patented his electro-magnetic telegraph, an instrument of high importance, since it afforded movement signals of various kinds, which could be applied to most important purposes. The "communicator" is the first part of this apparatus deserving attention. A thin disc of wood, turning horizontally upon a pillar or axis, has its circumference divided into equal spaces, alternately filled up with metal or ivory. The metal divisions communicate with a central column, and through it with one pole of a battery, of which the other pole is connected with the return wire, or with the earth. Against the circumference of the disc rests a spring, from the foot of which proceeds a wire going to the line or long conductor. As the disc is revolved on its centre, the spring rests alternately on metal and ivory, and were there no break in the magnetic circuit at the distant station, the current from the battery would be transmitted or intercepted accordingly. Over each division of the circumference is placed a letter or figure, so that, by bringing one letter after the other opposite a stop fixed near to the disc, the galvanic circuit would be opened and completed alternately with each succeeding letter. For the ease of turning the disc, it is provided with spokes or arms, radiating around its upper surface.

The telegraph operated upon by this "communicator," possesses great simplicity both in its principle and construction.

Opposite and near to the poles of a temporary or voltaic magnet, is placed a small armature of soft iron. When the iron is rendered magnetic, the armature is attracted to it; but, on interrupting the galvanic circuit, the magnetism of the iron ceases, and a small reacting spring throws the armature back to its original position. The armature itself turns on an axis, which carries a pair of pallets, taking into the teeth of an escapement wheel and moving the wheel onward, one tooth at a time; or a spring barrel and fuzee are employed to turn the escapement wheel, and the pallets merely control its revolutions, like the same parts in a common clock. The object is to communicate to a light paper or mica dial, bearing letters around its circumference, a step by step motion, wholly under the control of the operator at a distant station; so that he may bring any figure or letter on the dial to a small opening in a screen, through which it will be visible to the observer. The number and order of the signals upon the paper disc, correspond with those on the "communicator," so that the operator sees on his own dial the signals he makes on his correspondent's apparatus. To reduce the chance of an error, each word, as it is completed, is acknowledged by the correspondent, through a signal, before the next word is commenced.

Two of the important applications of the principles of this invention of Professor Wheatstone, must be mentioned. The multiplication of "telegraph clocks," to any number, by their connexion through a single wire with one governing chronometer at a central point, so that the indication of time, in every part of a country, might be the same precisely; and a contrivance for enabling the telegraph to print its own intelligence, instead of rendering it visible, or to do both at the same time. For the latter purpose a type disc is made to rotate, precisely as the paper dial or the index would do, in front of a cylinder covered with white paper; there being interposed between the type and cylinder, a sheet of the copying or transfer paper well known as the carbonic ink paper. The slowness with which signals would be rendered, as compared with the needle instrument, has prevented this grand invention of Wheatstone's from being, as yet, brought much into use. Mr. Bain has also distinguished himself by successive inventions of an improved electric clock and telegraph; but neither have these been brought into general use.

In 1843, Mr. Cooke introduced the most important improvement, regarded in a commercial point of view. This was the suspension of the wires, in the air, upon posts or standards, for insulation, instead of conveying them under ground. The wires do not come in contact with any part of the standard, but pass through rings of earthenware. Iron wires of a large size can thus be used, instead of copper, and the cost of constructing a telegraph reduced one-half.

The needle instrument, from the great rapidity with which messages can be sent, has hitherto obtained the preference over Professor Wheatstone's electro-magnetic telegraph, in England; but the latter is in use in France, and has there been entirely approved of. Within the last few years, too, a great and important improvement has been introduced into Wheatstone's invention, by the use of the electric current derived by induction from a permanent magnet, instead of the voltaic battery. This plan is not applicable to the needle instrument, but is peculiarly so to the electro-magnetic telegraph.

The extent to which the Electric Telegraph has been brought to bear in England, may be judged from the fact that, at the present time, about two-thirds of the railways already constructed are supplied with telegraphic wires. The result is the establishment of a complete system of communication between every important town in the kingdom with a central office in the metropolis, adjacent to the Bank and Royal Exchange, at which the whole telegraphic news of the country is concentrated and forwarded in every direction. Independantly of the immense advantage which a system like this presents to the government and the trading and commercial classes of the country, it has the advantages of being conducted on such a moderate scale of charges as to bring its beneficial influence within the reach of private individuals, who, for a few shillings, may transmit a message containing twenty words something like a hundred miles in the course of a few seconds.

DIAL PLATE ELECTRIC TELEGRAPH.

Vizetelly Brothers and Co. Printers and Engravers, Peterborough Court, 135 Fleet Street.

www.ingramcontent.com/pod-product-compliance
Lightning Source LLC
La Vergne TN
LVHW050151060326
832904LV00003B/113